STREETS AND TRAILS OF THE YORKSHIRE DALES

Settle • Giggleswick
Malham • Grassington

STREETS AND TRAILS
of the
YORKSHIRE DALES

Settle • Giggleswick
Malham • Grassington

Jennie
Crawford

Wharncliffe Books

First Published in 2000 by
Wharncliffe Books
an imprint of
Pen and Sword Books Limited,
47 Church Street, Barnsley,
South Yorkshire. S70 2AS

For up-to-date information on other titles produced under the
Wharncliffe imprint, please telephone or write to:

    Wharncliffe Books
    FREEPOST
    47 Church Street
    Barnsley
    South Yorkshire S70 2BR
    Telephone (24 hours): 01226 - 734555

ISBN: 1-871647-72-X

A CIP catalogue record of this book is available from the
British Library

Cover illustration: Mitchell Lane from Castleberg, Settle

Printed in Great Britain by
Redwood Books, Trowbridge, Wiltshire

CONTENTS

'To Roger'

Road over the tops from Settle to Airton.

*I*NTRODUCTION

STREETS AND TRAILS OF SETTLE, GIGGLESWICK MALHAM AND GRASSINGTON.

Ancient townships in three different river valleys each have a special identity, yet share a fascinating history. Linked in the past by old green lanes and monastic tracks running over the wild moor tops, a common history unfolds of Celtic tribes and Norse settlers, drovers and packhorse trains, sheep farmers and miners. Ancient routes contour the limestone outcrops, high above the valleys, past Bronze Age burial mounds and hut settlements, before descending to reach the sanctuary of hamlet or township.

If these routes had names, they are lost in time. There were very few street names before medieval times: this was because each dwelling in a small community would be known by the name of the occupant or owner, a tradition continued in the names of Grassington's Folds and many of Settle's Yards.

Monastic track from Prior Hall, Malham, to the beck crossing at Beck Hall.

Streets and their Names

By Seaty Hill, near Malham Tarn, there is the curious name of 'Street Gate', a point where important roads cross. We are used to the main road in a town being 'High Street', but this 'street' could hardly be more isolated. In fact, the word 'street' is Anglo-Saxon in origin, and means a paved road, (being often used for an important or Roman road), whereas 'gate' comes from the Danish word for a street, being commonly found all over the north of England.

In the past, a 'lane' was a less important thoroughfare (as in Back Lane, Malham and Moody Sty Lane, Grassington), whereas the word 'road' is fairly recent, being only used from around the fifteenth century.

Before the Industrial Revolution, most street names were descriptive, like Finkle (or crooked) Street in Malham and Mire Lane, Grassington, or were derived from local field names, like Ingfield Lane in Settle.

After the Industrial Revolution and up to the end of the nineteenth century, many streets were named to celebrate civic achievements or famous personalities, and so in Settle we have Station Road, Albert Street and Victoria Street. In the twentieth century, avenue, drive and crescent became popular, linked with names of trees and flowers to give a genteel rural ambience, and more recently mews and court are favoured by developers wishing to convey upwardly mobile aspirations!

Today, Settle is a bustling market-town with tranquil back roads and alleys and Giggleswick its refined neighbour with mellow church and famous school. Malham is a beautiful village, alternately peaceful or hectic depending on the tourist season, and Grassington a much-visited historic township, whose cobbled lanes are steeped in history and worn with the tread of miner and mill worker.

The names of streets can help to unearth some of the long forgotten history of each township and its environs, bringing past into present. In the fascinating study of streeet names, most are open to interpretation; questions are many, and reliable answers few.

This short book cannot be comprehensive, but is hopefully a starting point containing enough of general interest to encourage the reader to

Ancient green way to the rear of Prior Hall, Malham.

The track winds across Mastiles and Kilnsey Moor

research further and, in particular, to consult the excellent books and leaflets by Arthur Raistrick, W.R. Mitchell, Ian Goldthorpe and others, whose commitment and research have enabled so many readers to explore the history of Ribblesdale, Airedale and Wharfedale.

The derivation of names, where appropriate, has been taken from A.E.Smith's *Place Names of the West Riding. English Place-Name Society, 1961.*

1 $\mathscr{T}$RACKS AND TURNPIKES

'What a delightful thing's a turnpike road'
From *Don Juan* by Lord Byron.

The history of the tracks and roads in mid-Craven is likely to begin with the earliest tribes who populated the upland areas. People of the Middle Stone Age are believed to have come to Malham Moor each summer, leaving flint instruments to be discovered more than two thousand years later. The limestone uplands around Settle, Malham and Grassington show evidence of the settlement of Bronze and Iron Age people, and the earliest tracks would probably link these settlements, keeping to the high ground away from the thick woods and swamps of the valleys. The Romans came and went, leaving a marching camp at Mastiles and possibly a road through Settle.

Anglian tribes formed farming settlements in the valleys and on well favoured slopes; the farms later expanded into townships such as Malham and Grassington. Norse settlers preferred to farm the higher ground, leaving to us names like Trenhouse (the house of the crane) on Malham Moor.

Between the thirteenth and sixteenth centuries, most of the land in the area belonged to the great monastic houses, especially the Cistercian Abbeys of Fountains, Sawley and Furness and the Augustinian Bolton Priory. The trackways over the fells would see the passage of people carrying out abbey business, travelling through to their properties in the Lake District, or visiting the granges (or monastic farms) such as Kilnsey and Malham, to collect dues at the many abbey sheep farms, or to organise the transport of wool back to Fountains Abbey, with ox-drawn carts labouring on the road over Greenhow Hill. The main business was sheep farming, but drovers also brought cattle from Scotland to the great annual fair at Malham Moor, and pack-horses carried goods to market at Settle and Grassington.

After the Dissolution of the Monasteries in 1539, the well-used pack-horse ways remained, and teams of up to forty pack-horses transported essential commodities between moor, town and village, over the upland ways.

At the same time, towns were gradually expanding and becoming more industrial, drawing in people from the surrounding countryside and further afield. Due to the appalling state of most through routes,

Thomas Jefferys' map of 1775

Turnpike Trusts were set up to improve roads and collect tolls, like the Keighley and Kendal (1754) and the Wetherby to Grassington (1758). In 1806, the list of trustees for the District of Road between Pateley Bridge and Grassington numbered over 300, being gentlemen from Skipton, Malham, Grassington, Airton and London.

Thomas Jeffreys' 'County of York Surveyed' map, drawn twenty-one years after the Keighley and Kendal Turnpike was set up, shows clearly the main connecting tracks between townships and villages, and how the turnpike took over in importance. The empty and desolate country over which the old upland tracks passed, is vividly apparent on the map which pictures a desolate and rocky landscape.

The properly surfaced toll roads at last made wheeled transport viable; the roads were less direct, but had far easier gradients. Pack-horse ways gradually ceased to be used and the sturdy jagger ponies, along with those who had depended on them for a living, would soon be gone for ever.

Wagon team near Settle

2 $\mathcal{S}$ETTLE

'...my friend; come take thy place on the settle
Close by the chimney-side...'
(from Longfellow's poem *Evangeline*)

Settle coat of arms.

Many visitors to Settle will be drawn to climb the path to Castleberg, the precipitous limestone crag which seems to overhang the town. From the flagpole at the top, a bird's eye view of the town takes in a wide panorama on a clear day, from Penyghent and Wold Fell (where the River Ribble rises), to Giggleswick Scar, Bowland and Pendle Hill. Far below, between the town's chimney-stacks and rooftops, are caught glimpses of archways, stone steps, narrow secretive streets, cobbles, cottages and historic houses. The route of the old pre-turnpike main road can be seen, winding through the town, crossing over Duke Street at the Market Place and heading towards Giggleswick across the river.

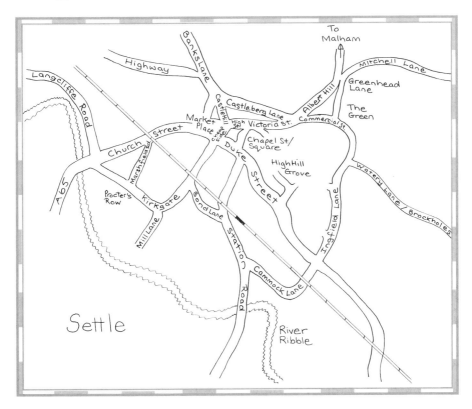

Reproduced from the 1896 Ordnance Survey map, 6″ to one mile.

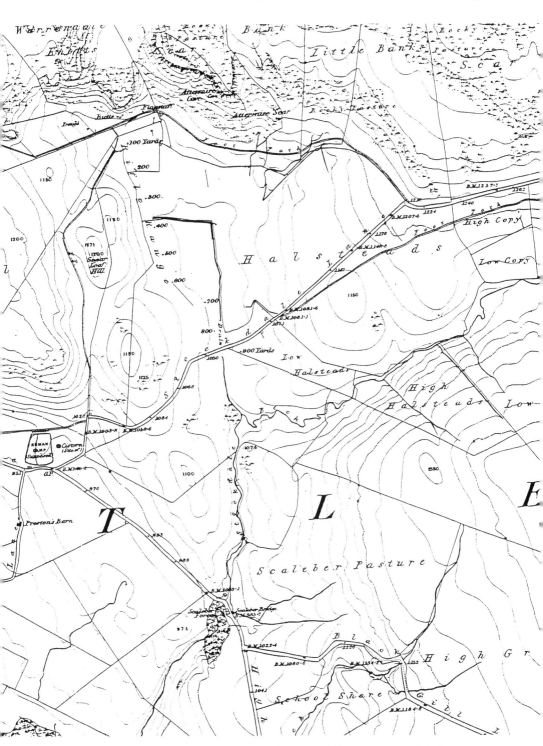

Settle and Upper Settle in 1896, showing the supposed Roman camp and the lane to Stockdale.

Early History

Settle is first recorded in the Domesday Book (1086). The name comes from Old English and means 'dwelling' or 'seat', while its close neighbour Giggleswick is likely to mean 'Gikel's village', or perhaps 'church village'. At the time of the Domesday survey, Settle and Giggleswick belonged to Roger of Poitou, but soon after passed into the ownership of the Percy family. By the end of the thirteenth century, however, much of the land in the area was owned by Sawley Abbey, and this continued until the Dissolution of the Monasteries in 1539.

Settle from Castleberg. The market place is clearly seen, with its traditional shops and inns, the 'Naked Man' facing on the left, the old through route runs to the left of the Town Hall, here called Cheapside to recall that it once bordered the market place. As Kirkgate, the way to the church at Giggleswick, the road continues beneath the railway arch and on towards the river.

A market has been held in Settle since 1249, and this has shaped the town's life and character, with lively Tuesday markets and fairs in April, August and October including Hiring Fairs, Goose Fairs and

Leather Fairs, which drew leather workers, traders and labourers from far afield. At fair time, the market-place would have been full of penned sheep and cattle, with many more waiting just outside town for their turn to be brought to market. At one fair alone, over twenty thousand sheep were shown.

The town's history is also closely linked with transport and the means of travel, from the days when the pack-horse trains came over the moors on rough tracks and green lanes, weighed down with panniers of salt, wool, coal and other commodities. Drovers brought sheep and cattle to market; local farmers brought their produce to trade and the town prospered with inns and businesses making a good living from folk passing through.

Many of Settle's houses were rebuilt in the seventeenth century, as can be seen from the many unusual door heads with dates from 1660 to 1690. However, Thomas Gray, the poet, visited Settle in 1769, and described the town's houses as "old and low, with little wooden porticos in front".

Early Streets
Some early recorded street and place names in the town were High Street, Highway, Kirkgate, Market Place (1655), the Marshe (1679), the Green (1706), Mill Lane, Settle Cross (1656), the Bond Lane (1812), Fishgate Holm and Shambles (1845 Tithe Award), Bond Lane and Butch Ing (1812).

Pre-Turnpike Roads
The old 'Red Judges' Road' followed a route from York to Lancaster and may be partly Roman in origin. Thomas Brayshaw, in his 1922 *Guide to Settle*, says that this road '...ran from Malhamdale, past Highside to a ford across the river, to a great extent following the line of the old Roman road' . It is said that this meant the Roman road between York and Lancaster.

The ancient highway over the moors to Long Preston measured by Ogilby may be easily followed and is a pleasant walk on a fine day. The road leaves Settle by Albert Hill, and turns into Mitchell Lane for a climb up onto high ground with extensive views towards Pendle Hill, before dropping down steeply to Long Preston. This would be a link in the route between the West Riding and Kendal.

Old Settle and The Green were once important as the first civilisation reached after a long trek over high moorland, and there was an inn on the Green, called the *Rising Sun*. Various trades and a tannery were grouped around the Green, as well as the original croft

The Folly in the past as Taylor's Refreshment Rooms.

The Folly, Victoria Street and School Hill today.

(from which Upper and Lower Croft Streets take their names).

The route of Ogilby's main road into town from Malhamdale and Long Preston ran down Albert Street to High Street, via School Hill (or Victoria Street), past the Folly, along High Street, and so into the Market Place, turning left before the present Town Hall (which replaced the Tollbooth in 1833), to cross directly over what is now Duke Street. Continuing along Kirkgate, the pre-turnpike road crossed the River Ribble either by the Ribble Bridge, which is thought to have been originally constructed in monastic times, or at Kendalman's Ford, and so to Giggleswick.

The town's orientation must have seemed very different compared with today; the *Golden Lion* faced onto the Market Place (in the building now a bakery cafe and Lambert's newsagent's shop), before it removed around 1754 to face onto Duke Street, the turnpike road which from that time onwards carried all the traffic.

The Turnpike Road

The increased need for transport of goods and people, and the deplorable state of the roads called for action and, in 1753, a Turnpike Trust was formed, after a meeting at the Talbot of house owners whose property was worth more than £3,000.

In 1754, the Keighley and Kendal Turnpike road was established, and communications were immediately made easier. The main reason for the turnpike was that larger quantities of wool needed to be transported from Westmoreland and Craven to the clothiers at Halifax market. Skipton became important as the wool collecting point for Craven. Toll bars were put into action, as at Runley Bridge.

The turnpike road opened up new opportunities for Settle. Fresh life and trade were brought into town as movement became possible across the country, and the first tourists were encouraged to visit the natural wonders of the area.

Some of the inns were by-passed by the new road, and gradually went out of business, whereas others - like the *Golden Lion* (which changed position to face onto the turnpike road) - were able to adapt and prosper.

In 1847, the craftsman shoemaker Titus Nelson of Cononley arrived in town. He had pushed his handcart full of shoemaker's equipment up the turnpike road and set up shop, first in Chapel Street and then in Duke Street where he stayed. The business prospered and adapted to new demands, first making coachmen's boots, then supplying 'navvy boots' for workers on the Settle to Carlisle railway line. The hobnail boots, with leather tanned in Settle, were taken up the line to the construction camps to sell.

Such businesses prospered and stayed in the same family for generations, giving a stability to the town's economy.

Coaching Days

After the construction of the turnpike road and before the coming of the railway, coach travel was supreme. The stagecoach ran on alternate days between Kendal and Leeds, horses being changed at the *Golden Lion* at midday. The inns did a roaring trade, with horses to change and visitors to accommodate. However, the coming of the railway was to change this before too long, and was said to be 'the ruination of innkeepers'.

The state of the turnpike road was a perennial subject of complaint: at an annual meeting of the ratepayers of Settle on 1 April 1854 it was objected that 'the Surveyor had spent too much upon the roads, and that they were not in a good condition...that the road from the north end of Settle to the Bridge had far too many stones upon it and that they were not sufficiently broken'. The surveyor explained that he 'had been given a quantity of stones and that people had complained of their lying too long at the roadside; and that having no place to lay them, he was obliged to break them up and lay them on the road'. However, the other side of the argument was put, (nothing being straightforward), that the surveyor 'had done good service to the town as Guardian of the Poor and had greatly diminished the Poor's Rate, by being enabled to employ Poor Persons on the Road'. Consequently, he was re-appointed for a further year at the old salary of £20 (13 to 5 being in favour!).

Meantime, the watch looked about the streets after dark, and mothers told their children scary tales of sinister apparitions stalking the streets at night. Warnings of the headless man of Barker's beck and the ghostly Scaleber-Trash, complete with clanking chains, would keep any youngsters from straying out after dark!

1851 Census: Streets and People

From the 1851 census return, it is interesting to see which streets and main buildings were included, particularly noting the many inns.

New Road	Market Place, *Royal Oak*	Market Place, *Naked Man*
Market Place	Market Place, *Crown Inn*	Eagle Street or Kirkgate
Kirkgate	Kirkgate, *Spread Eagle Inn*	Bond End
Eagle Yard	Duke Street	Duke Street, *Joiners Arms Inn*
Duke Street, *New Inn*	New Street	The Terrace
Marshfield		

'End of the Town of Settle'

Anley House	Anley Lodge	Runley Bridge
King's Mill	Procters Row	Bridge End
Church Street	Constitution Hill	Town Head
Castlebergh Wells	Chapel Square	Back Stables
Back Lane	Town Hall	Top of Shambles
Folly Hall	Low Gate	High Hill
Upper Settle	Green Upper Settle	

For comparison, on the 1851 Ordnance Survey map, the principal names are as follows:

Old Road	Bolland's Lane
New Road	Butch Lane
Cammock Town Field	Brockhole Lane
Mitchell Lane	Banks Lane
Mill Lane	

The Census gives a fascinating picture of the people who lived in the town at this time - their occupations and families.

At the Town Hall in 1851 were three households, being nineteen people altogether. The head of the first family was a master saddler, his wife engaged in domestic duties, an unmarried daughter worked as an assistant librarian and seamstress, a son (widower) being a saddler, a scholar grandson aged thirteen and a granddaughter aged eleven (domestic duties).

The second head of family was a linen and woollen draper, whose wife and daughter were shop assistants.

The third family's head was a railway goods clerk, his wife a school-mistress, his daughter an assistant school-mistress and six lodgers were listed (a dressmaker aged nineteen, a house servant aged forty-five and four scholar children).

Occupations of those living at Top of Shambles were overlooker in cotton factory, labourer, several power loom weavers (cotton), two cotton rovers, a bookbinder, railway clerks and a porter, master tailor and apprentice - and all their families!

Finally, we inspect the *Royal Oak*, where Henry Ayrton lived, innkeeper and farmer of thirty acres, his wife and six children with ages from two to nine, two visitors (mechanics born in Liverpool and Douglas, Isle of Man), an ostler and two household servants.

Yards and Alleys

Settle's many 'yards' are a special curiosity, the oldest dating from the seventeenth century. Some were courtyards for the town's many inns, like **Commercial Yard** off Duke Street, built in 1774 as stabling and accommodation for the Commercial Hotel, with a tunnel to a further yard used for horses. **Talbot Yard,** the stabling area behind the *Talbot Inn*, is thought to be the earliest. The inn was also known as *The Dog*, the connection being the Talbot dog - a local breed used by the drovers. Coach-horses would most likely be watered at Well Steps, round the corner. The **Delaney Court** development stands on the site of the *Golden Lion's* Back Stables Yard. Bishopdale Court was originally called Back Kirkgate Yard, and the large warehouse style building which is still there was formerly a house, some parts dating from the seventeenth century, with nearby seventeenth century weavers' cottages. This may have originally been the yard for the *Golden Fleece*, another Kirkgate inn left stranded by the turnpike.

Other yards took the name of the builder or owner, containing work premises and tiny cottages

Off Market Place.

Talbot Yard.

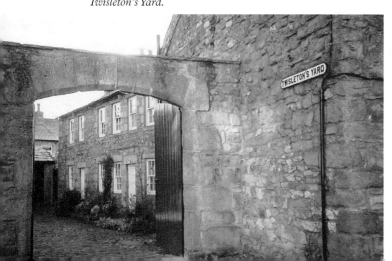

Twisleton's Yard.

Bishopdale Court.

Chapel Yard.

Bowskills Yard.

Commercial Yard.

Castle Hill.

which often had stone steps to the upper floor. Some of these named yards are **Bowskill's Yard, Howson's Yard, Tatham's Yard, Radcliffe's Yard** and **Twisleton's Yard** (where there was one water pump for all fifteen cottages). Some say that the yards were originally built for protective reasons, against Scottish raids, as in Kendal. It is true that the entrance is often through an archway, which could be closed off if required. However, most of Settle's yards are of later date than the Scottish raids, but possibly still built with protection in mind - from the weather, wandering animals or perhaps from vagabonds and rascals attracted to the markets. Dark canyon-like alleys are also to be found in unexpected places off Kirkgate and Cheapside.

STREETS OF SETTLE

Albert Hill
Albert Hill leads into Victoria Street. The old route into Settle from Malhamdale, Long Preston and further afield passed along Albert Street or via The Green, and continued down Victoria Street or School Hill. The street is named in honour of Albert (1819 - 1861), the Prince Consort of Queen Victoria.

Banks Lane
From Old Danish for a slope, Banks Lane climbs over 'The Banks' (or Castlebergh Pasture) as shown on early maps. This is the Settle end of the 'Monks' Way', a medieval monastic route from Settle to Langcliffe and Stainforth.

Bond Lane
The name is likely to come from an Old Norse word 'bondi', meaning peasant landowner or unfree tenant. Around Settle, and very clearly around Malham, can be seen on the hillside evidence of the Anglian farmers who created cultivation terraces or 'lynchets', the strips being owned in turn by different villagers. Another name for the strips is 'bombeys' which again derives from the Old Norse word. A further name used widely in the area is 'reines', which may be noted in Raines Road, and also Raines Lane in Grassington.

Cammock Lane
From a British word 'cambo' meaning crooked (or elbow-like), the lane runs alongside what was Great Town Field. 'Cammock' is the name of the steep hill and escarpment around which the River Ribble

winds at that point. Cammock Lane, Station Road and Bond Lane were previously Bollands Lane (a reference to nearby Bowland, where on the Jeffreys map of 1775, Bolland Knotts describes Bowland Knotts west of Settle).

Castleberg Lane or Highway

The word Castleberg or Castlebergh means 'castle hill', the word 'berg' or 'bergh' being from Old English or Norse.

From Castleberg Lane, a steep path leads to the top of the craggy limestone precipice called Castlebergh - a superb vantage point for looking over the town, the lower slope being a well loved excursion and picnic spot from Victorian times, with children's amusements and refreshments provided. At special times, swing boats were in evidence, with dancing bears, escapologists and other entertainments in the market place. It is thought that the summit of Castlebergh once had defensive works (as suggested by the nearby street Castle Hill).

Old print of Castlebergh, with a gentleman standing in rather a precarious position.

Folklore even suggests that the whole escarpment was used as a sundial in the eighteenth century, four stones being positioned on the lower slopes, and this could be seen for several miles to the west.

At the junction of Castleberg Lane and School Hill is an old milestone built into the roadside, marking distances: 236 miles to London, twenty-six to Hawes, sixteen to Skipton and twenty-six to Lancaster. These distances are in 'Yorkshire miles', which are longer than normal miles! - the reason being that before the eighteenth century, some places still used 'customary miles' rather than statute

Milestone in the wall on Castleberg Lane.

Chapel Street and Liverpool House.

miles, which were adopted in 1593.

Another name for Castleberg Lane is Highway, the high route which skirts the town centre. The old main road entering Settle forked at the bottom of Albert Hill. It is believed that the road followed Victoria Street, by Primrose Farm. However, it is interesting that a London and Lancaster milestone forms part of the wall at the junction of Highway with School Hill. Highway is an old through route to Langcliffe via High Road, a back way along the top of the town, which gives a fascinating view into nooks and crannies of yards and alleys.

Chapel Street/ Chapel Square

The street is named after an earlier Wesleyan Chapel. Chapel Street is off the main thoroughfare, and this perhaps follows a tradition of nonconformist chapel building in unobtrusive places, (so as not to draw unwelcome attention to chapel-goers). Liverpool House (built in the mid-eighteenth century, and formerly two houses) stands at the corner of Chapel Square, where there was a small pool in the vicinity, known as Paley Puddle; (the Paleys were a well respected local family, whose main residence was in Langcliffe). This was intended to become a canal basin for a planned extension to the Leeds/Liverpool canal, but was thought in the end to be not commercially viable and therefore never built.

Cheapside

The name is Saxon in origin, and means 'market', often referring to a general market area. Dr. Benjamin Waugh, founder of the National Society for the Prevention of Cruelty to Children, was born in a cottage formerly standing at the junction of Cheapside and the Market Place.

Cheapside and Castleberg from Kirkgate.

43786. SETTLE: CHEAPSIDE & CASTLEBERG.

Church Street (formerly New Road)

Church Street is named in honour of the interesting Victorian Parish Church of the Holy Ascension, built by Thomas Rickman in 1837. The church is unusual in that it stands north/south instead of the usual east/west. The Ribble Bridge used to carry the pre-turnpike road over the river, and is thought to date from monastic times. It was extensively repaired by the West Riding in 1662, widened and improved around 1754 (for the turnpike) and 1837, and rebuilt in 1958.

Commercial Street

Victoria Street, Albert Hill and Commercial Street are often found together, and usually mark an area of importance for a town, named in honour of the Queen and her Consort. At one time there would have been many little shops and trading premises in this area, now all residential.

Craven Terrace / Craven Cottages

The name is likely to come from a Celtic word for the wild garlic found growing in this area. In the Middle Ages over fifty places in the upper Aire valley were recorded as being 'in Craven'.

Duke Street

The original name was Duck Street or Duck Lane before the turnpike road was built, and it is said that a large duck pond was sited in nearby marshy ground. However, it is commonly

Duke Street, then and now.

upheld that the name was not thought grand enough for the main thoroughfare, hence the change to Duke Street!

On the road out of town towards Long Preston, a seventeenth-century mile post may be seen near the Turnpike House, registering thirteen miles to Skipton, one mile to Settle and seventeen miles to Clitheroe.

Greenhead Lane and The Green

Steep and narrow, Greenhead Lane winds down to the Green between old houses, from the Malhamdale and Long Preston roads. The Green area was once much more important when traders, flocks and pack-horses travelled through on their way into Settle. The placing of Greenhead and Greenfoot implies a larger green area than the one we see today: perhaps this would have been necessary for tethering horses and collecting together the livestock for market. The word comes from Old English for a grassy spot or village green. Upper Settle was bypassed when the turnpike road was built, but must once have been a busy and thriving community. There was a tannery and an inn called *The Rising Sun* on Albert Hill.

It is said that two gallows stood on the Green and later, more cheerfully, a maypole.

Lower and Upper Croft Streets date from the mid-nineteenth century and were built on land belonging to a farm called 'the Croft'.

The Green.

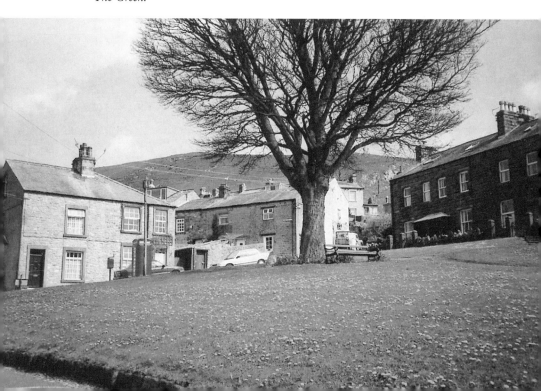

High Hill Grove
High Hill Grove looks out onto the 1,300 ft High Hill (first recorded in 1651).

High Hill Lane
High Hill Lane, the ancient pack-horse route to the moors, is also shown on the 1896 Ordnance Survey map and rises with an alarming gradient along the slope of High Hill, to continue past Scaleber Force waterfall: there is a supposed Roman camp on the left just before the turn off to Stockdale. A pinfold - where straying animals were impounded - was built at the junction of the roads to Long Preston and Malhamdale by the landlord of the *Golden Lion*, as recompense for extending his stables over the old pinfold, when his inn removed to Duke Street to take advantage of the turnpike. The pinfold is now restored as a delightful picnic spot, in memory of Mrs Kathleen Knights who served the Settle community faithfully for many years.

High Street
A town's main road was often called High Street in medieval times. *The Talbot*, one of Settle's oldest coaching inns, is on High Street, as was also the *King William IV*.

Ingfield Lane
Ing Field was the land bordering Ingfield Lane and what is now the *Falcon Manor Hotel*. The word 'ing' usually means meadow pasture or, as likely here, watermeadow. The lane was previously called Butch Lane, which probably means 'abutting strips of land'. The more romantic meaning of 'archery butts' is preferred by some i.e. the place where the townsfolk did their archery practice.

The *Falcon Manor Hotel* was previously a Victorian residence called Ingfield House, and was built in 1842 by G. Webster for the Reverend H.J. Swale, first vicar of the Church of the Holy Ascension, Settle.

Kirkgate
The name comes from the Old Norse word for 'church', together with 'gata' which is used commonly for roads leading to a particular location. This road led to the parish church in Giggleswick, which served the community as the parish church for Settle too, until 1837. It is said that a Roman road lies on the same course, and crosses the river by the ancient ford, just below King's Mill.

Kirkgate was also known as Spread Eagle Street, from the *Spread Eagle Inn*, a large hostelry on the old through road, which covered the area of Procter House and its surroundings. Victoria Hall dates from 1853, and claims to be the oldest surviving music hall in the country. It was built on the site of the old National School, before it moved to School Hill.

The Friends' Meeting House is also on Kirkgate and dates from 1678.

There used to be a tradition in Settle that every Shrove Tuesday a rough football match was held in Kirkgate, with large numbers of folk joining in the fray - a chance to sort out old scores!

Langcliffe Road

From the Old English for 'long cliff', this is an apt description of the situation of Langcliffe, where the long hillside bordering the valley ends in a limestone escarpment.

Market Place

Permission was given in 1249 to hold a Tuesday market, and this has brought travellers, farmers, drovers and tradesmen to the town and shaped its character from early times. The Shambles is the unusual arched market building with houses on top. The word originally meant a booth or bench. Later it was taken to be a place where meat was cut up and sold. Dating from the seventeenth century as an open market hall, arches and cottages were incorporated in the eighteenth century, and a second storey added at the end of the nineteenth century.

The Town Hall stands in the Market Place and was built in 1832 on the site of the old tollbooth. The watchman's room and town lockup were on the same site. Below the road are said to lie the remains of the town dungeon. John Wesley preached in the Market Place on the 4 June 1777.

The *Naked Man* was originally an inn (with a *'Naked Woman'* at Langcliffe!) - the name is thought to poke fun at the excessive fashions of previous days.

Marshfield Road

This is another name which describes boggy ground in the area, marshes being a feature of the land around this section of Kirkgate and the River Ribble.

Marshfield House, from which the road takes its name, is a dignified eighteenth century building, built by Thomas Salisbury of

A steam fair in the market-place contrasts with an old photograph of market stalls and parked vehicles. The Market Cross and Shambles both stand out.

Newton in Bowland whose wife was from Settle's Lister family. About 1790, it was reputed to be a headquarters for the making of base coin, a reference to the illegal activities of 'coiners', groups of local men who would secretly shave the edges off coins and melt them down to make more money, an underground practice well known in Yorkshire at that time. There is a legend that from the house, a secret passage ran to the river.

Mill Lane

Leading down to Kendalman's Ford and the footbridge, Mill Lane reaches the impressive King's Mill, formerly Procter's Mill. The mill was converted to cotton spinning after its earlier uses for the manufacture of snuff, and as a corn mill.

Mills in the area preferred to use readily available water power if possible, as coal was of inferior quality, and needed to be brought some distance, from Fountains Fell or Ingleton, transported on pack-ponies.

Mitchell Lane

The lane climbs out of Settle from Albert Hill and Greenhead Lane, to gain the tops. This is the old main road from Long Preston to Settle and, although now a pleasant walk in good weather, must have been a very different undertaking for travellers on a foul night with driving sleet, before the coming of the turnpike.

Procter's Row

Named after the owner, this row of terraced cottages was built for the mill workers in 1833, and features an archway through to the backs (now blocked up, but still visible). See also Mill Lane.

Sandholme Close

The meaning is a sandy water meadow (from Old Norse).

Station Road

The first Settle station was what

Mitchell Lane from Castleberg.

is now Gig;gleswick station, (where travellers might have been forgiven for thinking they had arrived in the middle of nowhere!) on the Skipton to Ingleton line (or 'Little North Western' railway), which was constructed in 1848. Station Road was laid down around 1849 to make access to Settle easier, and ran across an iron toll bridge over the Ribble, called Penny Bridge, because the toll was one penny! The road's course was from Beggar's Wife Bridge to Duke Street, taking in the middle part of what is now Bond Lane and Cammock Lane, and involved demolition of the New Inn public house, which stood opposite Cragdale House (now the police station).

Twenty years later, a new line was constructed from Settle junction right through the town, and the famous Settle to Carlisle line, with all its spectacular engineering, was born.

Town Head (Avenue and Way)

Town Head is named after a notable Victorian private residence.

Victoria Street

Born on 24 May 1819, Victoria was Queen of the United Kingdom of Great Britain and Ireland from 1837, and also Empress of India from 1876. Her reign was the longest in English history, encompassing tremendous changes and advances in science, technology, exploration and the arts and almost every town throughout the land has celebrated her, and often Prince Albert, in one or more street names.

Where Chapel Street meets Victoria Street stands The Folly, an ancient building thought to date from 1675, and a source of fascination due to its different decorative features and building styles. It is said that the house's curious name probably came about when it was left empty for a number of years in the eighteenth century. Others suggest that the owner was financially over-ambitious with the scale of his project! Previously, the name was 'Tanner Hall', after the profession and source of revenue of its original owner, Richard Preston.

Watery Lane

A watercourse draining from the fields flows suddenly and surprisingly along

Watery Lane.

Watery Lane, before disappearing into the fields on the other side. The track is also called Brockholes Lane (meaning 'badger holes'). The lane is followed to Mear Beck, which means 'boundary stream': an appropriate name as the stream in question runs along the Long Preston boundary.

Well Hill

The pathway leads up along the side of the Folly to three stone troughs, with old stone steps (Well Steps) up onto the Highway. A hillside spring used to feed the troughs, which were used from early times for household purposes, smithy work and for watering animals. At the time of going to press a welcome project by Craven Conservation Group will hopefully restore the water system in the near future.

Thirsty animals, having travelled the arduous exposed moor road from Long Preston or Malhamdale, must have welcomed the well's refreshing waters at the end of a long day!

Illustration from Horner Collection of   *Well Hill Steps today.*
Girl on Well Hill Steps.

3   *G*IGGLESWICK

'At Giggleswick, where I a fountain can you show,
That eight times a day is said to ebb and flow'
(from Michael Drayton's '*Polyolbion*'. 1613)

arly spring afternoon in Giggleswick, and the sun glows upon the mellow stone of St Alkelda's Church and alike upon the fine old yeomen's houses, whose secret gardens are sheltered by high stone walls and visited by frog, heron and long-tailed tit. Ducks fuss in the beck which flows under the clapper bridge carrying an ancient road, an inn's stone niches reveal a surprising secret and an Ebbing and Flowing Well intrigues the curious visitor. History records the now sleepy village echoing to the footsteps of Scottish raiders and Roundheads, seeing the passage of travellers and pack-horse trains and counting Samuel Pepys, Captain Cook, Nevison the highwayman and Edward Elgar among its famous connections.

Protected from violent westerly and northerly gales by the massif of Giggleswick Scar and the slopes of Buckhaw Brow, the village with its church and little River Tems lies in a sheltered position, raised above the marshy Ribble lands: from early times good sheep farming land, but with very little space for growing grain and cereal crops.

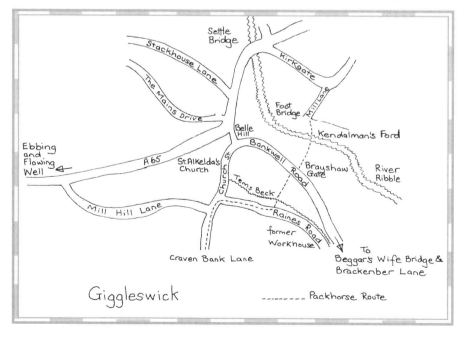

Reproduced from the 1896 Ordnance Survey Map, 6″ to one mile.

Near Giggleswick School Chapel, looking up the Ribble Valley, with the village and St. Alkelda's Church in the middle distance.

Early history

Giggleswick is recorded in the Domesday Book (1086), later spellings being Gykeswik (1204), Gekeleswik (1221) and Gigilswyke (1423). The name is likely to mean 'Gikel's dairy farm', this interesting personal name meaning 'icicle' in both Norse and Old English. The ancient parish of Giggleswick covered a wide area and until 1836 included the townships of Giggleswick, Settle, Rathmell, Langcliffe and Stainforth.

It has been suggested that Giggleswick parish lies on an important Pennine east-west route, which was used from prehistoric times. Did men of the Stone Age bring stone axes this way from the 'factory' on the Langdale Pikes - and did a Roman road pass this way? Certainly

Old view of Giggleswick Village from Cammock Hill, Settle. Giggleswick School Chapel stands on the hill to the left of the picture.

Clapper bridges over Tems Beck, past and present.

remains have been found at Skipton, Long Preston and Ingleton, together with the 'camp' at Settle and another on an ancient track above Knight Stainforth.

At the time of the Domesday survey, William the Conqueror had given the land of Giggleswick to Roger de Poitou, and it was recorded that 'In Ghigeleswic, Fech had four caracutes for tax', (a caracte being approximately 100 acres, and Fech's family presumably Lords of the Manor from pre-Conquest days). In the twelfth century, the land passed to the great

On the route of Ogilby's highway - crossing Tems Beck.

Percy family as overlords. It was William de Percy who founded Sawley Abbey and oversaw the gift of Malham Moor and Tarn to Fountains and Stackhouse to Furness.

Later, Lords of the Manor assumed the name 'de Giggleswick'. and continued to give to the great Abbey foundations. Adam de Giggleswick among other benefactions gave Furness an annual sum for 'providing veils for the heads of those who came to the Abbey gate to be treated for ringworm'. Giggleswick suffered at the hands of the Scottish raiders, with well documented attacks in 1138 and 1319, when the wooden houses were all burnt down and the village folk would have fled to the nearby hills and caves for safety.

The pack-horse 'short cut' from Settle towards Kendalman's Ford.

Ancient Routes through Giggleswick

Ogilby's succinct description of Giggleswick leaves few descriptive clues about the old road through the village:

> 'At the end (of Settle) whereof over a stone Bridg you enter Giggleswick, a village of 5 Furlongs and some Entertainment: of Note formerly for several small Springs here found, that Ebb and Flow almost every quarter of an hour. Leaving Gigleswick, you ascend an Hill of 8 Furlongs, and descend again 4 Furlongs, and pass by a Village and Lakeland Hall on the left...'

We can assume that all wheeled transport from Settle - and those wishing to avoid a dip in the Ribble - would travel down Kirkgate, swinging round to reach the bridge, up the steep hill to the present turn off the A65, and so down Belle Hill into Giggleswick village. Continuing along Church Street, the road would have crossed the Tems Beck at a clapper bridge, to

Kendalman's Ford today: the river bed and banks have changed and would have been easier to negotiate in the past.

Kendalman's Ford is in the middle distance.

The pack-horse route leaves the river.

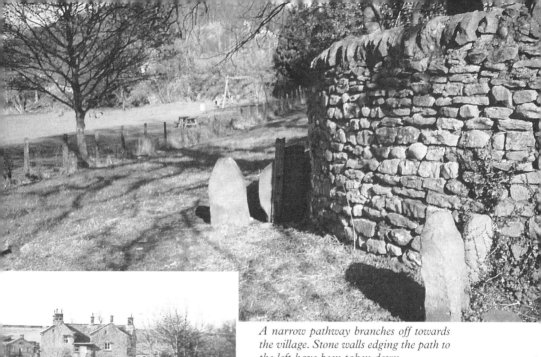

A narrow pathway branches off towards the village. Stone walls edging the path to the left have been taken down.

rejoin the pack-horse route at Beck Hall. The highway would then climb Craven Bank Lane on the way to Lawkland Green and Cross Streets near Austwick. Pack-horses with their heavy loads, and animals to and from Settle market were able to take a different route, crossing at the ancient Kendalman's Ford. It was thus possible for them to avoid Giggleswick village completely, together with the steep hill up from the river.

This route is likely to have

The pack-horse route skirts the village.

Pack-horse route at Raines Road.

turned off Kirkgate by the present Fire Station, and reached the Ribble downstream of King's Mill, along the narrow track which has been left between two industrial areas. On the Giggleswick side of the river, a walled lane carries the old track past houses and across Bankwell Road, to continue across the Fellins field past Armitstead Hall and, according to Brayshaw, back onto Ogilby's Highway near Beck Hall.

The Turnpike Road

Ogilby's highway was the main route through Giggleswick until approval was given in 1753 for a new road, the Keighley to Kendall turnpike, the present A65 trunk road. It was ordered on 19 July of that year that *'The Turnpike shall be carried under Giggleswick Scarr and over Brunton and not through Lawkland'*. Since the village centre was now effectively by-passed, and just as the *Golden Lion* had done in Settle, the *Harts Head* removed round the corner to a more

"The Turnpike shall be carried under Giggleswick Scarr and over Brunton..." the A65 heads towards Giggleswick and Settle in quieter days.

A65 'Turnpike Road' with Post Horn Books and the 'new' Hart's Head.

favourable trading position fronting onto the main road.

Toll bars were tried at each side of Settle Bridge - at the Langcliffe Road and Stackhouse Lane junctions in turn, but did not last long as they were a financial disaster; locals found them easy to avoid and would charge travellers for helping to find their way round!

Today, another by-pass, built in 1988, speeds fast traffic past Settle and Giggleswick, on the way between West Yorkshire and the M6, and again has had a huge impact on the character of the town and village.

Footpath between Settle and Giggleswick.

1851 Census: Streets and People

From the 1851 census return, streets and dwellings of Giggleswick are listed: the date refers to the first record of this name.

Gildersleets	Station	Craven Inn
Swabeck	Close House	Field Gate
Grain House (1585)	Rome (1561)	Wham
Sandforth Brow	Routster (1652)	Longridge
Low Paley Green/High	Paley Green (1593)	Croft Closes (1771-Cross Closs)
Huntworth (1606)	Catteral Hall (1403)	Craven Bank
Holiwell Toft (1845-Croft)	Beck House	Stackhouse (Domesday Book)
Thames Street	Ivy Court	Belle Hill
Hart Head	Holme Head	Settle Union Workhouse

Many other residents were listed simply under Giggleswick. Village folk followed a wide range of occupations at the time of the census. The following are some recorded:

hand loom weaver, power loom weaver, farm labourer, railway labourer, grocer, shop work, printer compositor, carter, school mistress, book keeper, gardener, cordwainer, carpenter, farmer and pauper.

At the station lived Thomas Morphet, railway station clerk born in Kirkby Lonsdale, Westmoreland and his wife Sarah from Settle. Their seven children were Thomas, Sarah, John, Mary Ann, Isabella, Jane and Robert, whose ages ranged from nineteen to two months. At the same address lodged James Payne, aged eighteen, a railway labourer and British subject born in the East Indies.

A large well-to-do family lived at Catteral Hall. John Hartley, Landed Proprietor, born in Sawley, and his wife Esther were in residence with their son, William (solicitor) and other children Mary and Ellen ('at home'), Esther, Elizabeth, John, Anne, George and Robert (scholars). Also living at the Hall were Christopher Cook (out door servant, born in Long Preston), Alice Greenbank (born in Horton in Ribblesdale) and Mary Kendall (born in Sawley) both house servants.

Streets of Giggleswick

Back Lane

The early 't'Back Lane' ran from the village towards Buckhaw Brow, later developed as part of the turnpike route, and it is on the Scar side of the Buck Haw Brow road that the remarkable Ebbing and Flowing Well is situated. It was remarked in 1760 that the Well had become 'the capital curiosity of the country'.

In the past the water was often observed to rise and sink every seven or eight minutes, its change measured from 'a few inches to half a yard' - and early observers attributed this to supernatural powers, with particular good luck for those who saw the 'silver thread' in the bottom. It was traditionally believed that the spirit of the well helped the highwayman Nevison to avoid his pursuers with a magic bridle: he was able to ride up Giggleswick Scars and through Nevison's Nick to freedom: also to jump Gordale Scar - an awesome feat.

Another tradition was for village children to visit the Well each Easter Sunday to make up liquorice water. In recent times the Well has also caused dismay to golfers, with ebbing and flowing flood waters on their course.

An old photograph of the Ebbing and Flowing Well.

The Bank Well.

Bankwell Road

The Bylaws of Giggleswick (1564 - 1602) provide

> *'That every inhabitant dwelling between the Church steele (stile) and Brayshaw geege (gate) upon reasonable warning given them shall come once a month to cleanse and scoure the* **well** *at the north of Thomas Bankes house in paine of every fault 3/4d'.*

Thomas Bankes came to Giggleswick from Feizor in 1564 and lived at The Well. His descendants continued to live at Bankwell throughout the seventeenth century, while a further branch of the family established themselves at Beck House. Ann Bankes of Beck House married Roger Pepys (cousin of Samuel Pepys) in Giggleswick Church, but she died a year after they were married. Joseph, younger son of Robert Bankes of Beck House, moved to Sheffield and was the grandfather of Sir Joseph Banks, President of the Royal Society and botanist on the *Endeavour* with Captain Cook.

Beggar's Wife Bridge

The name is first recorded in 1580 as 'Beggar wathe', meaning 'the ford where beggars waited (for alms). The word 'wife' was a later addition to the name - to give some fanciful interest!

A tale is told about a beggar's wife, who was murdered by her husband and returned to haunt the spot. Her fearful ghost was described as 'a rushing shape with nothing but a cobweb for her face'.

The 'old' Hart's Head - past and present cottages.

Belle Hill

Local people believe that the name refers to a bell which was rung to warn of Danish invasion. There are other possible meanings: the (Celtic) Hill of the Ford, the Hill of Baal (Druidical connections), Baile Hill (was a castle here?), reference to a bell which guided travellers over Kendalman's Ford, or maybe even a hill with a beautiful prospect - a case may be made for all.

The old *Hart's Head Inn* may still be seen as three private cottages on Belle Hill, one of which is called Garstangs after Robert Garstang and his family, who owned the coaching inn for many years. On the arrival of the turnpike road in 1753, Robert decided to build a new *Hart's Head* round the corner on the new route, (in the same way as the *Golden Lion* at Settle had switched its position). The old *Hart's Head* has a colourful past, being the secret headquarters of the local Jacobites in

Belle Hill - Ogilby's route into Giggleswick.

the early eighteenth century, complete with a secret escape route in a cupboard by the fireplace.

Earlier, in 1665, the imprisoned Quaker George Fox was transported between the castles of Lancaster and Scarborough, and was guarded as he rested overnight at the *Hart's Head* - in his words, the guards '*...had me to Giggleswick that night, but I was exceeding weak. There they raised the constables with their clog-shoes, who sat drinking all night in the room by me, so that I could not get much rest.*'

At the end of the nineteenth century, the property (Cravendale) was bought by the famous local doctor Charles Buck, musician and great friend of the composer Edward Elgar. The pair would ramble happily over the limestone country, larking about hunting 'cats' on the scar, and on one occasion losing a parrot from its cage on Settle Bridge!

Brackenber Lane
The name is first recorded in 1303 and comes from Old English and Old Norse words for bracken and a hill or knoll. A 'Holy Well or Plague Stone' is marked on the 1896 OS map, situated nearly opposite the *Craven Inn*. This is likely to be an old boundary stone, of which two others were found on roads out of Giggleswick.

Plague swept the country in the years around 1590 to 1599 and boundaries of infected areas would be marked. The 'Plague Stone' was where food and other goods would be brought and left for those within the area. Money for payment was left in a water-filled hollow in the stone, to try to contain the spread of disease.

Brayshaw Gate
The point where the pack-horse trains crossed Bankwell Road from the river is known as Brayshaw Gate, and the name refers to the gate at this spot which kept animals out of the village! Queen's Rock House on Bankfield Road has been the home of the Brayshaw family for centuries.

Church Street
A Saxon church may have stood on the spot where St Alkelda's Church is built. The present building is over 500 years old, with traces of Norman architecture to be found. The Saint's name is most unusual: there is only one other church in the country dedicated to St Alkelda - at Middleham, Yorkshire. The legend of the Saxon Saint's martyrdom relates how she was strangled by Danish women, for her faith. This name has also been suggested as meaning 'Holy Well' after several nearby. The church has been severely damaged

St Alkelda's Church, Lych Gate and the old 'Market Cross' with children, some in bonnets. Postcard sent on 18 April 1905.

The same scene today.

several times in its history, during the Scottish raid of 1319 and during the Wars of the Roses. During the Civil War, Colonel Lambert's troops were billeted in the church, and remains of their fires have been found. The church has been a place of refuge throughout its history, demonstrated by a huge oak beam which can be fixed across the door inside.

The old 'market cross' is rumoured to have been taken from Settle, and is a reminder of a long-standing dispute going back to the thirteenth century. The quarrel was between members of the Percy family who had a conflict of business interests over competing mills in Settle and Giggleswick. To cut a long story short, Giggleswick folk were upset when Settle was granted a market

St. Alkelda's Church.

The Black Horse.

Tems Beck and ducks.

Church Street.

The Hearse House on Church Street.

charter in 1249. The matter was still gently simmering in 1784, when a visitor remarked on hearing a local story that Settle had 'stolen a market from Giggleswick'.

The *Black Horse* public house is thought to have been closely linked with the church in its Roman Catholic days, and contains two niches which may have held statues of saints.

Craven Bank Lane

As with Craven Terrace in Settle, the name Craven recalls the wild garlic found all over the area. St Awkeld's Holy Well, covered over since 1866, rises nearby, and flows into Tems Beck (referred to as 'Thames' in the 1851 census - a word thought to mean 'black river'). A Giggleswick bylaw (1602) was instituted to keep the well pure, stating *'That none shall lye and ffish or fflesh or any other Hurtfull thing to steepe it St. Awkeld well in paine of every time 4d'*.

Giggleswick School was founded in 1507 by James Carr of Stackhouse. The domed chapel in its magnificent position was

Giggleswick School Chapel.

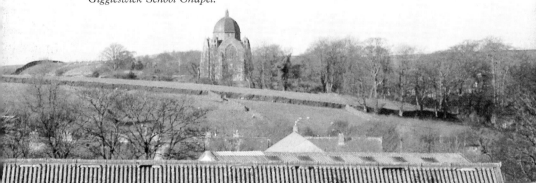

designed by T.G. Jackson and built between 1897 and 1901, a gift to the school from Walter Morrison of Malham. Morrison was very interested in the exploration of Palestine - hence the idea for a dome on a Gothic building. Jackson was thrilled to have the chance to design and build a dome and was determined '...*to show that domes and Gothic architecture are not incompatible, and, though I shocked all the purists, I am not dissatisfied with the result*'.

Ancient lane past the chapel.

The ancient school tradition of 'Potation Day' (12 March), was an annual fair day when scholars received figs, buns and ale and the governors and masters retired to the *Hart's Head* for a meal and liquid refreshment. Cock fighting was held in the school yard.

The Mains Drive
From Middle English, the word means demesne (domain) or land - usually belonging to the lord of the manor.

Mill Hill Lane
Mill Hill Lane takes its name from the nearby Mill Hill, the ridge near Catteral Hall. Giggleswick's corn mill was situated on the Tems flowing from Giggleswick Tarn, very close to Catteral Hall, and was used for cotton towards the end of the eighteenth century until its demise.

A Giggleswick bylaw (1564 - 1602) stated '...*That noe inhabitant of G. shall grave any sods upon the mill hill except for repaireing of the butts in paine of 6s 8d*'. The butts were archery butts where shooting skills were practised. Butts Lane, off Raines Road, is where the butts were likely to be situated.

Raines Road
'Raines' or 'reines' are local words for the lynchets or cultivation

Raines Road, outside the old workhouse.

strips formed by ancient farming methods. This street name is quite common in the area, in places where roads were built over the 'town fields' as villages expanded. 'Brayshaw Reins' is the hillside behind the old workhouse. On Raines Road stands what was the workhouse, dating from 1834, and used jointly with the earlier Settle workhouse which was situated on Albert Hill, below the Catholic Church.

In 1841 the workhouse had 180 inmates. Ten years later, there were eighty-nine inmates, and their ages ranged from two months to eighty-nine years. The Workhouse Master was Thomas Brigg, with his wife Mary as matron, and their unmarried children lived with them: Betsy (dressmaker), Thomas (painter) and Ann (housework). John Bond, Workhouse School Master, of Barnsley, also lived there. Many of the inmates were listed as 'pauper', but others had followed a wide range of occupations: marble cutter, weaver-cotton, weaver-linen, shoemaker, butcher, factory hand, plasterer, servant, agricultural labourer, rail labourer, blacksmith, carpenter, joiner, tailor, plasterer, carter, school mistress, cordwainer, grocer and printer compositor. It is sobering to imagine so many people, in such a beautiful place, all fallen on hard times and unable to support themselves and their families.

Stackhouse Lane

From an Old Norse word meaning 'ricks', we can imagine a house with hayricks in the nearby fields. Around 1160, Adam de Giggleswick gave Furness Abbey *'a caracute of land at 'Stacus', together with rights to feed swine in Giggleswick wood, to cut timber for building and to use the common pastures of Giggleswick and Stackhouse.'*

The monks of Furness farmed at Stackhouse and built a corn mill by the river, causing an upset with the Settle mill: the resulting dispute was resolved by the Pope's Legate, Pandulf, and in 1221 the monks were granted an annual payment of 1lb of cumin or 2d and released of their 10s rent for Stackhouse in compensation for giving

up the mill. The Carr family of Stackhouse founded Giggleswick School and lived at the Old Hall for many generations, until the house was sold in 1950.

Typical Giggleswick doorhead.

4 *M*ALHAM

'...the stones of the brook softer with moss than any silken pillow, the crowded oxalis leaves...scarcely a place where one might not lay down ones forehead on their warm softness and sleep.'

(from *Proserpina* by John Ruskin)

The eagerly anticipated first view of Malham Cove from a rise in the road up-valley from Kirkby Malham is a magical moment for the many visitors who flock to this beautiful historic village in its unique setting.

Following in the footsteps of Charles Kingsley, (who wrote part of the *Water Babies* while staying at Tarn House), John Ruskin, J.M.W. Turner, William and Mary Wordsworth, the poet Thomas Gray, David Hockney and many others, all the 'Wonders of Nature' so much admired by Victorian tourists must be appreciated: Malham Cove, Gordale Scar and perhaps a visit to Janet's Foss, before tea by the beck.

In the evening quiet, the village and surrounding moorland take on an air of timelessness: the ancient paths and trails once trodden by people of the Iron Age, monks, drovers and labourers hold their secrets well, yet by looking at the names of streets and trails, some of the area's history is revealed.

Early History

The name 'Malgum' is recorded in the Domesday Book (1086). It is accepted that the township was named after Malce or Malcas, the leader of the Anglian tribe who settled here in the seventh or eighth century, so that the name would mean 'the place of Malcas' clan'. However, there are also several translations from

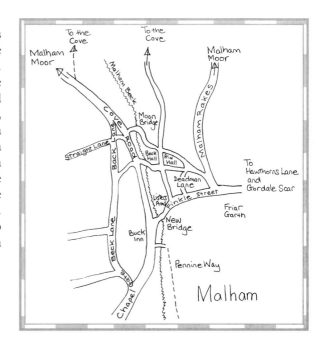

Field patterns to the east of Malham Cove.

Old Norse - the most interesting of which is 'sack' or 'bag', or 'place near the hollows'. In aerial photographs, the Cove takes on the appearance of a deep hollow or bowl - or even the front of a workman's apron. Other Old Norse meanings are 'a gravelly place' or 'sandbank'.

The original village is likely to have expanded from one or two farm settlements, to a group of wooden thatched dwellings facing

Malham Cove. *The made-up path to the top of the cove is seen on the left. Malham Beck flows down the valley from the foot of the cove, bordered to the east and west by ancient field systems. Several torrential floods have been recorded where water has burst over the top of the cove in a spectacular waterfall.*

onto the Green, and the original Malham Hall stood where the reading room is now, near New Bridge.

The thirteenth century was a time of great expansion for the monastic orders, as gifts and endowments allowed them to become powerful landowners. Sheep farming was the main business in the Malham area, and Fountains Abbey owned large tracts of land including Malham Moor and Fountains Fell. Malham township was divided into east and west, along the line of the beck. East Malham originally comprised twelve oxgangs of land, given by Helt Mauliverer to the Augustinian Priory and Convent of Bolton. It is believed that Prior Hall was the main grange (or monastic farm), with possibly Friar Garth as a secondary house. Malham West belonged to the Cistercian Fountains Abbey, with various grants of land by the Percys, Malhams and others. It is thought that Malham Hall and Old Hall (now Beck Hall) were Fountains' principal houses. As Beck Hall lay in Malham East (i.e. Bolton Abbey territory), the scene was set for considerable friction between the two monasteries, which lasted for many years until the matter was at last resolved amicably.

From a poll tax survey of 1379, the township of Malham numbered twenty-six married labourers and their families, five craftsmen and their wives, thirteen servants and an innkeeper. The main purpose of Malham folk, whether or not under monastic rule,

Rustic view of Malham showing the Cove and beck.

has been to make a living from the land; evidence of this is seen everywhere, from the Anglian lynchets or cultivation terraces near the cove, to the ancient field tracks and paths, leading from the west side of Malham out into the common fields and up to the copper, calamine, lead and iron mines on Pikedaw Hill.

A well-favoured spot for settlement: seen from the Cove fields Malham village sleeps in its peaceful hollow in the hills.

Beck Hall *(east of the beck) seen from the old lands of Malham West. The present day Beck Hall is thought to stand on the site of a much older property belonging to Fountains Abbey, called Old Hall. This would have been in the middle of land belonging to Bolton Priory, a potentially awkward situation.*

Malham Beck *in monastic times the dividing line between Malham East (mainly owned by Bolton Priory) and Malham West (which belonged to Fountains Abbey). Prior Moon's bridge can be seen in the distance.*

Early Roads and Tracks

The Jefferys map of 1775 shows the road up Malhamdale from Kirkby Malham, entering the village just past Tan House and leaving by three routes. What is now the Cove Road divides, with the left hand fork rising towards Ryeloaf Hill and Stockdale Edge, thence to Settle (on the course of a minor Roman road it is said), the right fork heading over Malham Coves (known now as Dean Moor), towards Malham Tarn, emerging onto the road past Low Tren House near the Water Sinks.

A second route leaves the village to the east of Malham Beck, (following the first section of Malham Rakes): however, the track then continues east of the cove (along Trougate), passing to the west of the Water Sinks, around Malham Tarn to Tarn Houses and onward to Arncliffe

A third route leaves Malham (by Finkle Street), to pass 'Gordell Scar' towards Lee Yate, Mastiles and Bordley.

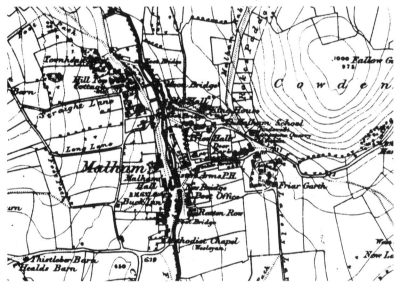

Malham in 1850. Reproduced from the 1847 to 1850 Ordnance Survey Map.

Malham Street Names in 1850

The following street names are indicated on the 1850 Ordnance Survey map:

Chapel Gate	Long Lane	Straight Lane
Malham Rakes	Finkle Street	Lavely Lane
Gordale Lane	Hawthorns Lane	Smearbottoms Lane

The old South View Café, at the junction of the Cove Road and Finkle Street. New Bridge and Lister's Arms Hotel can just be seen on the right.

An old view of Malham village, in the days before South View Café. Malham Beck flows peacefully beneath the clapper bridge by the blacksmith's.

It is interesting to compare the Jefferys routes with those on the 1850 Ordnance Survey Map, which is more detailed and shows a maze of footpaths and lanes, particularly to the north and west of the village. The two previously mentioned tracks which emerged on the moor

just south of Malham Tarn are now marked as 'footpaths', one over Dean Moor, the other over Prior Rakes via Slippy Stones, while the present route from Malham to Street Gate, (not marked on the Jefferys map, although this might mean that it was merely of lesser importance), makes an appearance as a 'footpath'.

From the 1841 census, we see a community of

Malham village's main road, seen on a quiet Sunday. The road rises to the right to cross the old pack-horse bridge and continues straight ahead as Cove Road, the most popular route to Malham Cove.

An old road past the Youth Hostel continues, crossing Priory Lane and winding onward, to give access to the eastern slopes and fields at the foot of Malham Cove.

Samuel Cowper's school at the foot of Malham Rakes.

varied trades and professions, with a large number of lead miners recorded. Other occupations were: farmer, agricultural labourer, joiner, gamekeeper, blacksmith, carpenter, cotton weaver, two innkeepers (Thomas Green and William Harrison), a schoolmaster (Samuel Cowper) and a minister, the Reverend William Richardson. The village's population at that time was 233.

MALHAM STREETS

Back Lane

Many villages with origins in medieval times have a 'Back Lane'. The name was used to describe a way which ran behind the village houses, forming a boundary with common or other land. This can be seen in Malham, where tofts and crofts are found in the land between the village street and Back Lane: two of these were Fish Croft and Corn Croft. A toft was the land a house was built on, and a croft was the piece of land or garden belonging to the house. Between the tofts and crofts, little tracks and lanes run from

Well used in the past, quiet Back Lane joins the Cove Road, the main access route for the many visitors each year. Malham Cove is seen in the distance.

Path to Hill Top Farm from Cove Road. The main entrance to the farm is on Back Lane.

the main street to Back Lane. These would have been more important earlier when the lane was in constant use for access north and west of the village, and into the fields or to the mines. Straight Lane and Long Lane are two tracks which start on the main road and cross Back Lane in order to go forward to Settle and to join what is now the Cove Road, and these are seen clearly on the 6″ Ordnance Survey map of 1850.

The seventeenth century Hill Top Farm, with its beautiful porch dove-cote was built by William Preston, whose initials are above the door, together with the date 1617. William Preston left money in his will for repairing the way between Settle and Malham and for building a one-arch bridge to replace the clapper bridge and ford at Monk Bridge (the bridge in the middle of Malham, now called New Bridge).

Chapel Gate

The portion of the main road leading into Malham from Kirkby Brow is called Chapel Gate. On older maps there can be seen a sharp bend just before the chapel. The road was very narrow, with high drystone walls and the bend was negotiated with great difficulty by larger vehicles and buses, before being straightened and widened to

Visitors follow the footpath to and from Malham Cove.

Iron Age field boundaries are revealed in the evening light.

form the present road into Malham, past the National Park Centre. The Methodist chapel on the left was built in 1865, with money raised by the people of Malham. A Methodist chapel is also shown on the 1850 Ordnance Survey map.

Cove Road

The Cove Road continues the main road to the west of Malham Beck, and takes the place of the old through route, Long Lane, which joins it about half a mile out of the village. The road goes past Calamine House, a storage place for the calamine (used in the making of brass), which was mined along with copper, lead and iron on Pikedaw Hill, mainly in the eighteenth and nineteenth centuries.

The road was formerly a footpath which led out onto Cove Pasture, the hillside south-west of the cove, where ancient ridge lines of Iron Age field boundaries can still be made out.

Crowds of visitors make the pilgrimage along Cove Road and the cove footpath to the echoing massive dry waterfall of the cove, nearly three hundred ft high, and a spectacular limestone feature. How many realise they are following in the footsteps of Celtic farmers two thousand years ago?

Deadman Lane

Possibly a macabre connection with the town gallows, Deadman Lane leads to Malham Rakes and so up to Shorkley Hill, where the

gallows were said to stand. In medieval times, a lane with this name often led to a burial ground.

In the area of Deadman Lane and Finkle Street is the Deerpark, where annual sheep and cattle fairs were held, many of the animals being driven for sale from Scotland. The annual Malham Fair, thought to date from monastic times, was an occasion for revelry and dancing in the village, with folk coming along from far and wide. In the eighteenth century, the fair gradually grew in importance and developed into the massive cattle fairs at Great Close on Malham Moor.

Route to the gallows or a burial way?

From the direction of Mastiles, Bordley and further afield, Finkle Street will have seen the passage of sheep, cattle, farmers and traders to the annual Malham Fair held on the Deerpark.

Finkle Street

This curious name is likely to mean crooked and winding, coming from a regional dialect word meaning 'bend' or 'elbow'. There is a Finkle Street in York (one of the narrow medieval shopping streets near the Minster), in Richmond, Sedbergh and other northern townships. Another interesting meaning is that of a road where fennel was sold. Finkle Street continues by Prior Rakes to Street Gate. However, in the past, the main route would turn east towards Gordale and Mastiles Lane, with branches off to the many tracks

Date stone built into the wall at the corner of Finkle Street and Deadman Lane. The stone, dated 1634, is thought to have come from one of the Lambert family's houses.

joining Fountains Abbey properties: Kilnsey, Bordley via Lee Gate (Farleegate), over into Wharfedale, via Malham Moor Lane (to Threshfield and Grassington), or a number of other tracks across Boss Moor and Threshfield Moor. After Gordale Lane, Finkle Street becomes Hawthorns Lane and Smearbottoms Lane (a reference to boggy ground rather than a quaint way to mark sheep!).

As in Settle, a Pinfold was needed to impound stray animals, and the outline of the enclosure can still be seen in the field opposite and a little uphill from the Malham cafe. The Pinder also used a small meadow called Pingring (short for Pinder Ing), off Lavely Lane. The village stocks stood in this area - just opposite the Malham cafe. Almost hidden in the wall at the corner of Deadman Lane and Finkle Street is a date stone showing 1634 and the initials W.L. (thought to refer to a member of the Lambert family).

The *Lister's Arms Hotel* was re-named after its owner, Thomas Lister who in 1797 became the first Lord Ribblesdale. The inn was previously called *'Dixon's'*, and is much older than the *'Buck Inn'* (on the other side of the bridge), which was built on the site of an older building by Mr Morrison of Tarn House, and named after either the local 'Buck' family - or the roe deer!

Gordale Lane
This is the portion of road leading from Finkle Street as far as Gordale House, (and thus to the Scar). The two parts of the word are most likely to come from the Norse for an angular (in this case, triangular) piece of land and a little valley.

The gorge formed by the collapsed cave roof, ending in a foaming waterfall, is a marvel of nature, viewed with awe by visitors - most famously Charles Kingsley, William and Dorothy Wordsworth and John Ruskin, while artists such as John Piper, James Ward, George Barret, Thomas Girton, David Hockney and Constance Pearson have found inspiration in its natural majesty.

Hawthorns Lane
The native hawthorn bush is seen everywhere in the Dales, along road sides and ditches, sometimes pleached into impenetrable

Approaching Malham from the south, a stunning view of the cove shows off its setting amongst the limestone ridge and high moorland.

hedges, or left to grow alone as a single tree, the wind bending its branches into tortuous shapes. The hawthorn has been used as a boundary for fields since Roman times and as a hedge since the seventeenth century. Fountains Abbey owned a house called Hawthorn Leys, thought to be Lee Gate further up the lane.

Kirkby Brow

The road to Malham from Kirkby Malham (meaning the church town of Malham), passes over the brow of a hill, from where there is a spectacular view of Malham Cove. Nearby are Aire Head Springs, where the stream out of Malham Tarn surfaces. The waters which emerge here go underground at Water Sinks, above the cove, but do not surface at the foot of the cove, as might be expected! The waters emerging at the cove are from a stream which goes underground by the smelt mill chimney on Malham Moor, together with other water draining from the area to the north of Pikedaw Hill. In very wet weather however, the two waters have been found to merge in the labyrinth of caves deep behind the cove. In exceptional rain and tempest, the flooding stream from the tarn at Water Sinks has been known to flow along the Dry Valley and over the cove in a spectacular waterfall with a vast cloud of spray.

Built to Prior Moon's order, Moon Bridge carried an ancient monastic track on the east side of the bridge. Remains of the 'Wash-dubs' may still be seen - this was where sheep were gathered and their fleeces scrubbed.

Long Lane

Long Lane was the original road up to Malham Moor on the west side of the village. The lane now joins the 'new' Cove Road half a mile out of the village. Between Long Lane and Back Lane there were crofts, for example Long Croft and Jamie Croft.

Malham Rakes

Raikes means the steep portion of a road. The 'Rakes Paddoks', shown on early maps, were the sheep enclosures all along the roadside. A sheep house belonging to Bolton Priory has been excavated in this area.

Moon Bridge

Just off the Cove Road, Moon Bridge (sometimes called Wash-dub Bridge, where sheep were scrubbed), the highest bridge upstream, is named after Prior Moon, last prior of Bolton Priory, who gave instructions for it to be built. It is a clapper bridge, (a bridge with stone slabs resting on supports), built to carry an ancient monastic track which ran from the direction of Bordley past Prior Hall, over the beck, uphill to join Straight Lane and onward to Settle.

Further downstream, another clapper bridge

The lane continues uphill from Beck Hall towards Prior Hall.

Beck Hall *clapper bridge and ford, an important crossing point of Malham Beck from monastic times. The bridge is now mainly used by tea-seeking visitors and horse-riders. Cromwell Cottage overlooks the stream.*

Previously called Monk Bridge, the old pack-horse bridge has been considerably modernised, having started life as a clapper bridge. Now its an excellent place to lean and contemplate the ducks in the beck (but mind the traffic!).

crosses the beck at Beck Hall (formerly 'Old Hall', the likely second house of Fountains Abbey, after Malham Hall), continuing on a second track from Prior Hall to Malham West. The present bridge of four limestone slabs resting on three piers possibly dates from the eighteenth century. The house by the ford is called 'Cromwell Cottage', a reminder of Civil War activity - and that Cromwell is supposed to have signed as witness for three weddings in Kirkby Malham Church. His friend John Lambert, who captured Bradford for Cromwell, lived in nearby Calton.

New Bridge

The main bridge over Malham Beck was formerly called Monk Bridge, and was a pack-horse bridge over the ford, originally a 'clapper bridge' thought to have been built by the monks. In 1636, William Preston of Hill Top left £6 in his will to build a one-arch bridge, and this was widened in the eighteenth or early nineteenth century to carry wagons. Over the years, further improvements have taken place to smooth out the awkward rise.

New Row

New Row dates from the seventeenth century, and it is said that the original Malham Hall, which was granted to Fountains Abbey in the thirteenth century, and would be their main house in Malham, stood on the land now occupied by the reading room and a shop. The second Fountains house was taken to be what is now Beck Hall.

Pennine Way

The Pennine Way, which runs from Edale in Derbyshire to Kirk Yetholm in the Borders was officially opened in 1965 at a ceremony near Street Gate on Malham Moor. Two thousand people witnessed the event: since then, thousands of walkers have tackled the 250 mile walk along the spine of England to Scotland, mostly breaking their journey at Malham Youth Hostel before tackling the next lap north past the tarn and over Pen-y-Ghent to Horton in Ribblesdale.

Priory Lane

This ancient lane ran from Prior Rakes, along the back of Prior Hall (some say the front - perhaps it depended which monastic house you

'Prior Hall' assumed site of Bolton Priory's main grange (or monastic farm) in Malham.

Green footpath passing to the rear of Prior Hall to go onward to Moon Bridge. Travellers to and from Fountains Abbey, with their animals, would perhaps be able to avoid Bolton Abbey property, on their way to Old Hall and Malham West.

The lane from Prior Hall continues as a steep downward track to the footbridge and ford at Beck Hall. This delightful way forms a green tunnel with dappled shade in mid-summer. Cromwell Cottage can just be seen through the foliage.

Over the Cove Road, the lane continues until it reaches Back Lane, then going forwards into the fields and hill pastures by several routes, including a path to Settle.

belonged to!), to the two lanes down to Beck Hall and the crossing of Malham Beck, either at Moon Bridge for Straight Lane, or at Cromwell Cottage. Prior Hall was thought to be the main house in Malham for Bolton Priory, with Friar Garth as the second in importance.

Straight Lane

Straight Lane is a continuation of the route from Moon Bridge, and is initially anything but straight! Going forward across the fields, there are several very old barns (or laithes) alongside, or very close

The Green Lane continues over the Cove Road from Prior Moon's Bridge.

Straight Lane at the junction with Back Lane.

Straight Lane and Pikedaw Hill, seen from Prior Hall

to the track. An interesting name is that of Burns Barn, which comes from Borrans, a name often used in the area of Roman camps or Iron Age fields. One could speculate that the name Straight might have originated as 'Street', a very old name for a paved way. The track rises to the boundary of the common fields and continues onward to Pikedaw Hill and Settle, where it emerges at Stockdale Lane, at the supposed site of a Roman camp. There are several Roman references here to fuel the dreamer's imagination.

5 *G*RASSINGTON

'Its Wood, Hills, River,Valleys,
And all its natural beauties
Have charm for me!'
(Grassington, April 1908
John Crowther, 'Botanist and Antiquary')

Grassington is recorded in the Domesday Book (1086) the early form of the name being Chersintone or Ghersintone, meaning 'grazing or pasture farm'. The village lies in a beautiful hillside situation on south facing slopes above the river Wharfe (a British word for 'the winding river'), protected from cold north winds. The first settlers chose with care this well-favoured spot, of which the Rev Bailey Harker several thousand years later extolled its 'hygienic features' to rival Ilkley's for ensuring health and speedy convalescence. The township's history is also linked with the development and demise of the Grassington Moor lead mines, and its subsequent popularity as an early commuter village for Bradford. Today the historic village is thriving, with a world famous festival, and has to cope with the pleasures (and pain) of tourism.

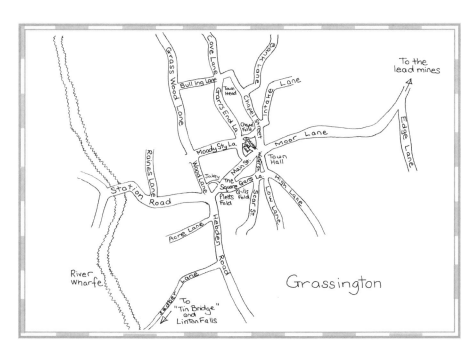

Reproduced from the 1894 Ordnance Survey Map, 6″ to one mile. Grassington Moor Lead Mines can be seen to the top right of the map.

Grassington from Grass Wood.

Early History

A large extent of limestone country to the north and north-west of present day Grassington, and including Grass Wood, shows much evidence of Iron Age settlements and walled field systems, perfectly placed and almost protected from view, continuing along the hillside towards Conistone.

The village we see today probably began, like Malham, in the centuries before Domesday, with one or two farms by a green, perhaps on the site of the Hall and the Square.

At Domesday, Gamelbar had three caracutes of land in Ghersintone. A hundred years later, Nigel de Plumpton was the first Lord of the Manor of Grassington, which was held by the Percy family from the King.

Many of the Grassington street names refer to land being taken in from waste (described as 'assarting' and 'intaking'), and farm land, and this will have occurred when the original farms began to expand - examples are Intake Lane, Bulling Lane, Garrs Lane and Tofts, all words describing enclosure of land from waste. This had mainly happened before the Black Death as, after this time, tenants had

Grass Wood.

more bargaining power for land, due to the decline in the population. There are reminders of the many small grazing paddocks and enclosures in street and place names such as Garrs End, Garrs Lane, Garrs Hill and Garrs Silva (now Grass Wood), while the northern entrance to the township was said to have been at Garrs End Laithe ('laithe' being the local name for a barn).

At the end of the fourteenth century, some thirty families were living in Grassington, including a shoemaker who kept the local public house and the interestingly named Adam Gawke (a Norse name for cuckoo). The township did not expand greatly for three centuries, there being

Prehistoric site in Grass Wood.

Footsteps of miners, tinkers, 'badgers' and shepherds, the ghostly Tinker's Lane from Hebden Beck to Edge Lane.

recorded only thirty-eight 'tenements' in the early seventeenth century, but all this was to change with the advent of industry in the revival of the Grassington Moor lead mines and the textile mills at Hebden and Grassington.

Early Streets
Some early recorded place names in Grassington (some later becoming street names) were:

Hardycrofte (1611)

The Garthe ende (1611)

The Hall, Griston Hall (Grassington Hall) (1685)

High Cross (1611)

Hissendene (1120), (Isingdale Beck/Bridge, meaning 'iron valley')

Lyeth landes, Lythe browe (1611)

The Withes (1589) (Wise House, meaning 'willow')

Early recorded names of fields are also interesting for their references to people or later houses and streets:

Blakeseckers (Blake's acres, 1611, from the surname)

Dowstones Coppy (Dovestones, 1611, possibly meaning dove or black stones)

Lane Side Field (Griston loane-head, 1671, meaning hill, valley head, river source or headland in the common field)

Mains (the Maynes, 1611, meaning demesne)

Mill Brow and Gates (Millyeat landes, 1611, meaning mill and an opening)

Scaleber Helks, 1717 (meaning rough, stony hillside fields)

Tofts (the Tofte, 1611, meaning 'enclosure')

Roads Up Hill and Down Dale
As previously described, ancient through routes kept high over the moor tops, or contoured the hillsides. High Lane is said to be on the approximate line of the route followed to Fountains Abbey from Kilnsey and the Malham Moor monastic properties and further from the west. The monks' route was agreed to keep to the edge of Grassington's cultivated land, away from the settlement; through Hebden, the line of the present B6265 towards Pateley Bridge carried ancient monastic, droving and trading traffic to Abbey lands eastwards, and later to the markets of York, Ripon and Knaresborough. From Conistone, a pony route ascends to Sandy Gate, also accessed from Grassington via Yarnbury, and this route can also be traced eastwards over the moor tops into Nidderdale.

Tinker's Lane passes New House.

Signs of an old through coach route north from Halifax to Richmond can still be made out on the west side of the River Wharfe, although mainly following the line of the present road.

Ruinous Roads and Turnpikes

The petition for a turnpike from Wetherby to Grassington in 1754, describes the road as 'ruinous and dangerous to Passengers'. In January 1756, the Coalgrove Head Company, mine owners, needed to transport a quantity of forty foot, (and one sixty foot) fir poles for their mine shaft. These needed to be brought in from the north, together with the necessary ironwork from Newcastle, and the carriers were recommended to come 'through Richmond on the direct road to Grassington' (possibly by Coverdale and Kettlewell) as the roads were described as 'excessive rotten' in the winter, (the usual route being via Ripon and Pateley Bridge).

In 1758, the Wetherby to Grassington road was converted to a turnpike, with a new lower line between Grassington and Hebden, the only Toll House between Grassington and Pateley Bridge being on Greenhow Hill. From Grassington, Jefferys' map shows the course of the road going forward via Skirethorns onto Mastiles Lane and the west. The old Conistone road continued on from Grassington to meet the road west of the river at Kettlewell.

The growth and importance of lead mining on the Grassington and Hebden moors meant that improvement in road transport was a major necessity. Easy access to the Leeds and Liverpool Canal at Gargrave was essential for the transport of lead, coal and lime. Although the Skipton to Grassington road had been much improved by the Duke of Devonshire, it was replaced by a turnpike road from Skipton in 1853.

Travelling was still hazardous, however, and in 1873, at Bow Bridge, on the road from Linton to Grassington, an accident occurred when a coach and horses went out of control on the corner at the foot of Great Bank, fatally throwing its occupants over the parapet and onto the rocks below.

The 1894 Ordnance Survey Map (see page 76)
The following lanes (and some places) are shown on the map: some of the lanes are out on Grassington Moor, and point to the past importance of the lead mines. Many old shafts are marked and named, such as Good Hope Shafts, Tomkins Shaft and Rakes Shaft.

Moody Sty Lane	Bull Ing Lane	Acre Lane
Sedber Lane	Scar Street	High Lane
Low Lane	Horse Gap Gate	Chamber End
Old Moor Lane	Mire Lane	Duke's New Road
Lime Kiln Lane	Bare House Lane	Intake Lane
Garrs End Lane	Cove Lane	Edge Lane
Bank Lane	Grass Wood Lane	

Alleys and folds lead to the rear of houses and shops, which were often extended and outbuildings converted to house the growing population of mine workers and their families. The Woggan (or Woggins, locally meaning a covered alley), was known as Crowther's Alley as it runs to the side of a building which was John Crowther's apothecary's shop (commemorated by a plaque on the wall).

1851 Census

The census gives an interesting insight into Grassington at a time when lead mining was still important, and the population was 1,138. Street and place names on the census include the following:

Hedge Side House	Losskill Bank House	Edge Side	High Cross
Edge Top	Gill House	Town Head	Mill Lane Head
Bank	Dawson Yard	Near the Chapel	Gill Fold
Moor Road	Hill Top	Rock House	Lythe House
Well Head	High Street	Plets Yard	Halfway House
Market Place	Garrs Hill	Listers Yard	Low Fold
Black Horse	Lee Fold	Scarr Street	Town End
Croft House			

Some of the family names on the census are reflected in names of folds and buildings or local names today. Some names listed include:
Brown, Harker, Rathmel, Tomlinson, Wood, Rogers, Simpson, Varley, Walton, Ibbotson, Wiseman, Metcalfe, Whitaker, Storey, Wiseman, Storra, Soakill, Bulman and Sidgwick.

Folds and Yards

Grassington's many folds and yards are a fascinating feature, often tucked away out of sight of the main thoroughfares, but forming an essential contribution to the village's history and character. Fold

Chapel Fold *(or Ranters Fold), showing the Primitive Methodist Chapel, built in 1837.*

Pletts Fold, *the house on the left is dated 1744.*　　***Chapel Fold***

names often celebrate local families whose names also occur elsewhere in the village. The folds were often originally farms and their yards and outbuildings. However, as the lead mining industry developed on the moor, experienced or out of work miners and their families arrived from mining localities as far apart as Derbyshire and Alston, and extra housing was desperately needed. Many folds developed to address this need, as larger houses and farms were divided, or outbuildings to the rear converted to miners' cottages. Many of the cottages in the folds date from the late seventeenth and early eighteenth centuries.

Dr Whitaker, writing in 1812, says that the miners 'contributed more to the increase of population than to the improvement of order and good morals'. However, this is contradicted by a traveller who in 1830 wrote that the miners were 'industrious and sober, putting all their money in the savings bank'. Their life must have been grindingly hard, some young boys already working above ground at the mines from the age of ten and often working alongside their fathers and brothers, and girls sometimes working in the mill from the age of eight, according to ages and occupations on the census returns. There being no other form of income, miners had to carry on working into their seventies and even eighties.

Summers Fold *also known as Ashfield.*   ***Hill Top Fold.***

The *Craven Herald* of January 1853 reports a fatal mine accident on the moor:

> '...as Thomas Rodgers was at work in the Beever Lead Mine, while attempting to make secure a large stone, it fell upon him and he was killed instantaneously...it is remarkable that his Great Grandfather, Grandfather and his mother's cousin, were all killed on the same Moor.'

Many of the folds and yards were named after occupiers or owners, and may have had several names at different times. **Chapel Fold** was also known as **St. John's Fold**, **Smith Fold** and **'Ranters Fold'** (a nickname given to the Primitive Methodists, whose chapel was built there in 1837).

Gill is a local family name, its meaning being 'a ravine'. Samuel Gill lived at Scawgill, a former small cotton mill at Town Head, at the

beginning of the nineteenth century, and at the 1851 census, a Gill family was resident at **Gill Fold.** Peter Gill, the head of the household was a carrier and farmer of thirty-five acres. Both he and his wife Isabella were forty-four, she being occupied with 'domestic duties', helped by his sister Mary, aged forty. Their four children were John (twelve), Elizabeth (eleven), Agness (six) and Francis (four) and all

Broughton Fold

were 'scholars'. A stepson, Thomas (twenty-two), employed as a carrier's servant also lived there and Thomas Ibbotson (fifty-eight), an agricultural labourer.

Pletts Fold is also named after a local family. Mr T. Pletts owned a laithe (the local word for a barn) on Water Street in 1890, still called Pletts Barn.

Brownes Fold was also named after a long standing Grassington family. In 1685, Stephen Browne supplied five casements for 12s 6d (63p) to help build a house at Conistone.

Rathmell Fold took its name from Jacob Rathmell who died in 1849. Rathmell's Farm was another name for Town Head Farmhouse, thought to be one of the oldest Grassington buildings.

Some other folds are **Ashfield Fold** (previously **Summers Fold**), **Hill Top Fold** and **Broughton Fold** which dates from 1754 and recalls a local family name - and the celebrated Grassington poet John Broughton.

Haunted Lanes and Village Pastimes

Although life could be grim, Grassington folk still found time for entertainment. Favourite sports practised were Bull and Badger Baiting and Horse Racing at Botton. Other lighter pastimes were Treacle Eating, Clock Dressing, Egg Throwing (at Easter), Churn Suppers (at the end of the hay harvest), Hen Giving (at weddings), Grassington Feast in October, in honour of St. Michael, and Copper Throwing, an activity where children scrabbled for coppers which had been heated in the fire, thus burning their little fingers, to the merriment of all (except the children).

As in Settle, ghostly apparitions were reported stalking the lanes at night. The Barguest with clanking chains roamed around Bull Ing, both Grass Wood and 'Tinkler Lane' were haunted and a spectral coach and hounds were often seen along Kirk Lane. A tale is told of one Charley Simpson returning home late one night along Grass Wood Lane. Thinking something was behind him, he quickened his pace until he was running in panic. Reaching Bull Ing, the noises stopped suddenly - but he did not, and fell headlong over the 'ghost' - Jackey Hargreaves' donkey which had been quietly trotting along the lane!

STREETS OF GRASSINGTON

Acre Lane

A way into the fields by the river, the word is from Old English or Old Norse for a plot of arable land, as in an acre of farm land. The original meaning was unenclosed land, later changing to tilled or enclosed land.

Badger Gate

Just across the river, on the Threshfield side of the bridge is the interesting name of Badger Gate (with Badger Lane not far away, near Burnsall). A badger was the name used for a travelling trader who had a licence to buy corn from the market and sell it on. Outlying farms and hamlets would be visited on his round, and he would often carry other small items like salt and spices (which were often used in the brewing of home-made ale). In different parts of the country, green roads are sometimes called Badger Gate or Badger Stile.

Bank Lane

The name is from Old Danish for 'bank, slope, river bank'.

Bull Ing Lane

Recorded in the 1846 Tithe Awards, the name is from the Old English word for 'bull' and an Old Norse word for 'meadow, watermeadow, pasture'.

Chamber End Fold *(previously King Street)*

A house in the fold is dated 1675, and is thought to have been at one

Chamber End Fold.

time both town council chamber and jail, which may explain this unusual name.

Chapel Street

Three chapels were built in Grassington in the nineteenth century, these being the Wesleyan Methodist Chapel (1811) in Chapel Street, the Congregational or Independent Chapel (1811) in Garrs Lane and the Primitive Methodist Chapel (built around 1837) in Chapel Fold.

Churchgoers, however, had to cross the river to attend Linton Church, as Grassington was part of the parish of Linton. This worked in good weather, but was not possible when the Wharfe was

Chapel Street. *Chapel Street and Town Head.*

Cove Scar.

in spate, so at such times, they used the chapel at Grassington Old Hall. At the far end of Chapel Street is Ingle Nook, with a datestone of 1628.

Cove Lane

The meaning is 'hollow in a rock, or cave', and this name appears frequently in the area . Cove Hole is nearby, with Cove Scar marked on the 1894 Ordnance Survey map, Cove Close and Heads in the 1846 Tithe Award and three Cove Laithes in the vicinity, not forgetting the famous Cove at Malham.

Cove Lane was sometimes called Fairy Flit, after the fairies said to live on the Cove. The ancient Fairy Hole is said to be a mound off Cove Lane, where 'fairy pipes' have been found. It was said that fairies lived in the quietest limestone recesses and there is a reminder of this at Malham, where the cave behind the waterfall at Janet's Foss is said to be the home of the Queen of the Fairies.

A further reference to fairies is in the name of Elbolton, the prominent hill seen across the Wharfe from Grassington, which means 'elf hill'.

Dales Way

This long distance footpath, a recreation route from Ilkley to Windermere via Dentdale passes through Grassington which provides a welcome stop for the night. The way borders the river before entering Grassington to follow Main Street, then heads out of town via Town Head and over Lea Green towards Conistone Dib.

Edge Lane
The name is from Old English for an escarpment. The lane is also a contender (with High Lane) for the line of the right of passage granted to Fountains Abbey, through Nigel de Plumpton's Grassington lands, and recent historians prefer this route, as being thought to be along the ancient division between cultivated land and waste.

Edge Lane - Where the cultivated land, taken from waste, meets the open moorland. Animals could be driven along here without encroaching on the landowner's private territory.

Garrs Lane, Garrs End Lane, Garrs Hill (and Silva Garrs - Grass Wood)
Garrs Lane was formerly Grassington's main thoroughfare, the word 'Garrs' being an old local family name, its meaning most likely taken from an Old Norse word for 'enclosure'. 'The Garthe ende' is recorded in Skipton Muniments of 1611. Further meanings of the word are a yard and a fishery, and there have also been suggestions that the word comes from the Anglo-Saxon for a spear, a meadow and one of the names of the sun god, Apollo!

An interesting cottage on the Lane, Theatre Cottage recalls Grassington's

Garrs Lane looking downhill towards the Square, Theatre Cottage is on the right.

GARRS END LANE

thespian history when, early in the nineteenth century, Tom Airey managed a theatre on this site, and attracted stage celebrities of the day such as Edmund Keen and Harriet Mellor. Grassington's theatrical tradition is still strong, carried on through the world famous festival, the Christmas Dickensian weekends and other events throughout the year.

Hardy Meadows
Hardycrofte is recorded in 1611, being the surname Hardy with croft, an Old English word for croft or small enclosure.

Hebden Road
Hebden comes from Old English and means 'hip valley'.

High Lane
The line of this road is reputed to be the ancient way used by Fountains Abbey, whose community was given permission, around 1190, to pass through Nigel de Plumpton's Grassington lands, on the way to and from Kilnsey and their other land and properties, as long as they kept to common land out of the village and beyond cultivation.

Intake Lane
The word is from the Old Norse for 'a piece of land taken in from waste', one of many such words describing enclosure from waste.

Jakey
There are several possible explanations to throw light on this curious name, which may be taken from the nearby Jacob's Fold. A more colourful explanation is that there were several old privvies (or jakes) close by the path.

There are many small pathways and alleys whose names are difficult to unravel: 'Lucy' by the *Foresters Arms*, Salt Pie Hill (perhaps where salt was sold), the ancient path known as 'The Woggan', and more recently Boiled Egg Row, a name for Bridge End, which has passed into folk history as the place of the putting on of tea-time eggs when the commuter train arrived at the station!

Main Street
Of the two thoroughfares descending into the square, Main Street is thought to have been the one of lesser importance. The street was previously known as 'Well Lane', a reminder that the stream from Well Head runs along its course to the pump in the square. At the top

Main Street. Views up and down.

of Main Street stands the Mechanics Institute, now the Town Hall and Devonshire Institute, built in 1855, and from here the narrow street threads down between folds, tiny shops and former yards through the square to Town End at the bottom.

The 1851 Grassington census reveals the importance of Main Street, which divides East and West Grassington as follows:

'All that part of the Township of Grassington which lies on the west of the Main Street from Simpson's Cottages at the top of the Town to Mr Wall's house at the bottom. Also the scattered houses on the North-East of Grassington extending from Bowdin's house on the Edge Side, to Grassington Moor and then to Gill House adjoining Coniston Township. (Total 488).'

'All that part of the Township of Grassington in the Parish of Linton which lies on the East side of the Main Street from the large Farm House at the top of the town to Mr William Cockshot's at the bottom. Also ... those few scattered houses on the South East of Grassington viz Mr Eddy's, Mill Lane Head, Low Mill, Lythe House, Half Way House and High Cross. (Total 600).'

The Reverend Bailey J. Harker published *'The Buxton of Yorkshire'* in 1890, a book celebrating Grassington and its environs. He writes in glowing terms of the beauty of the district but is less than complimentary about the Mechanics Institute Clock. 'The Public Clock is utterly useless', he writes and proceeds to compose a poem about it! The building which was Tom Lee's smithy stands on Main Street, and the tale is still told of how he murdered a local doctor, and threw the body into the Wharfe above Burnsall. He was later hung on a gibbet at what is still known as Gibbet Hill in Grass Wood, the scene of the crime.

Ashfield House dates from the late seventeenth century, and is likely to have been a farmhouse which later formed three lead miners' cottages.

Mill Gate

Grassington's Mill Lane can still be seen as a sunken road leading down to Low Mill by the river. A manorial corn mill once stood on this historic industrial site, and also a seventeenth century lead smelt mill founded by George Duke of Cumberland, Lord of the Manor. The textile mill was active from around 1840 and it is said was used in turn for worsted spinning, silk and cotton manufacture and soap making.

Close by are the stepping stones to the beautiful medieval Linton Church, reputedly haunted by the ghost of a monk.

Moody Sty Lane

This curious old name is wrapped in mystery. The way climbs over lynchets up from the river, so 'sty' can be taken to mean 'ladder', but this is one of the names whose origins are difficult to trace.

Moor Lane and Old Moor Lane

Moor Lane is an occupation road, or a road which goes out over rough land which has been taken into use, often for industrial activity. It leads to the large area of disused lead mines on Grassington Moor, once the scene of great industrial activity. The Brigantes and later the Romans are thought to have mined lead on the moor, and signs can be seen at Lea Green of early open-cast pits used in the fifteenth century. The main boom time for the lead mines was between the mid-seventeenth and mid-eighteenth centuries, after which there was a decline and final collapse of the lead market towards the end of the nineteenth century. In 1760, over 600 tons of smelted lead were produced from the Grassington Moor mines, and it has been estimated that an astonishing 5,400 horseloads of lead, 7,000 horseloads of ore and 4,000 horseloads of coal would be needed to achieve this. The effect on the state of roads and on Grassington itself, of this amount of traffic passing through can only be imagined. The ponies would need fodder, accommodation and

On the Duke's New Road.

minding, and many farmers hired out their horses to the mines.

Duke's New Road, off Moor Lane is a mine road named after the Duke of Devonshire who was Lord of the Manor of Grassington in 1750 and developed the lead mining industry on the moor.

Raines Lane, Raines Lea and Raines Meadows

The local word 'raines' refers to the lynchets or ancient hillside farming strips in the common fields, which are seen very clearly around Grassington and also around Malham and Settle. The name is often used where residential roads are built over former strips. This name may also be derived from the Old English or Old Norse for 'raven'.

Scar Street *(also Scar Lane and Scar House)*

Scar Street, leading onto Water Street, is thought to have been the course of a Roman road which crossed the Wharfe near Linton Church on its way north. The word is from Old Norse meaning a scar or rocky downward slope.

Sedber Lane

The name probably comes from an Old Norse word for a flat topped hill, and the path crosses 'Sedbur Field', an old arable field. This walled and paved lane, also known as the Snake Walk (from its

appearance) and the Flags (from the stones laid onto the previous muddy lane), goes downhill from the village to the footbridge over Linton Falls to the Birkbecks' worsted Linton Mill. The bridge (built by the Birkbecks in 1814, along with the footpath and kissing gate, to assist their workers' passage to the mill), was previously known as Tin Bridge because the walkway was covered with tin from oil drums, to protect the surface from the mill workers' clogged feet. Replaced in 1860, 1904 and 1989, the bridge is now expected to last until 2100 at least!

The arched pack-horse bridge seen in the field beside the mill is known as Little Emily's Bridge, and dates

Scar Street is said to be Roman in origin, and leads down past the Grange, whose name suggests links with monastic times.

Linton Falls in 1915, showing the "Tin Bridge" and weir.

Sedber Lane or the Snake Walk. Follow the paved path to Linton Falls and 'Tin Bridge', with riverside walks in each direction.

from the fourteenth century, when this was the route through to Linton Church. Little Emily is likely to have been the orphaned daughter of Christopher Norton (executed after his part in the Rising of the North), who was then raised by the miller at Threshfield Mill.

The Square *(previously the Market Place)*

In 1282, a Market Charter gave permission to hold a market each Friday and a fair at Michaelmas.

In 1812, the *Yorkshire Gazetteer* records Grassington as having no market, but fairs were held for horned cattle on 4 March and 26 September, and for sheep on 24 April and 29 June.

Church House, at the lower end of the square, has an interesting history. Dated 1694, it is thought to have been the family home of Stephen and Alice Peart. In the eighteenth century the house became a livery stables and later the Chapman family worked the business. For a while, the house became a temperance hotel and finally the church bought and consecrated the building in 1924.

The top of the Market Place was called Tan House End, from a tannery once there. On this site was developed the imposing Liverpool warehouse, selling all manner of goods and luxuries, which were now obtainable in the village, thanks to the Leeds and Liverpool Canal and the improving road and rail transport systems.

Grassington Post Office, the Square. Postcard sent from Doll to Flossie (c1920s).

After the First World War, this became the *Cafe Royal*, serving a growing clientele of out of town excursionists and cyclists as Grassington's attractions became well known.

One of the features which makes Grassington so attractive, is the orientation of many of the houses, whose gable ends are seen, rather than their fronts, described by Reverend Harker as being 'In curious and fantastic style'.

The Square today.

Black Horse Hotel.

Grassington

There were four inns in 1890, these being the *Commercial Inn* at Town End, the *Devonshire Arms, Foresters' Arms*, the 17th century *Black Horse* (previously known as the *King William the Fourth* and also the *Prince Albert*) and the Temperance Hotel. Many unexpected corners of the town have been hostelries at one time or another, with names such as the *Commercial Inn*, *Robin Hood* and *Jobbers Arms*.

Liverpool Warehouse and Devonshire Hotel.

Station Road

Station Road crosses the seventeenth century Grassington Bridge (previously called Linton Bridge).

At the beginning of the seventeenth century, the old wooden bridge was said to be 'ruinous' and oak trees were used to repair it. Further repairs were carried out in 1661 and 1780 when the bridge was made wider, and the old hump-backed bridge, having weathered the passage of thousands of pack-horse trains from the mines to the canal at Gargrave and Skipton, was finally substantially rebuilt in 1825.

In the vicinity of the bridge, pilgrims once visited a clear spring with healing waters, called 'Our Lady Well'. Lady Well Cottage dates from the sixteenth century and may possibly have housed travellers and pilgrims.

Grassington and Threshfield station was opened in 1902, bringing new life, and commuters to the village after the demise of the lead mines. There was a plan to extend the tracks to Kettlewell, but this was never done and the line was closed to passengers in 1930.

Water Street

A likely continuation of Scar Street (thought to be Roman in origin), the course of the two streets is a reminder that the Romans mined lead at Greenhow and also farmed the area

The cobbled lane is seen from Pletts Barn (the Mountaineer) where John Wesley preached.

for grain, needed for feeding the garrisons at Ilkley and Bainbridge.

'The Mountaineer' on Water Street is in the renovated building known as Pletts Barn, which may date from the sixteenth century. Another name for the barn was 'Wesley Barn', since John Wesley is said to have preached there in 1780. He mentions a visit to Grassington in his journal, when he preached at Skipton in the early morning, Grassington in the middle of the day and Pateley Bridge at night.

Wharfeside Avenue (Wharfe View)

The River Wharfe, which flows into the Ouse, is first recorded in 963, and is probably from a British word for 'the winding river'.

Wood Lane and Grass Wood Lane

Wood Lane out of Grassington continues as Grass Wood Lane past Netherside Hall in the direction of Conistone.

The mainly seventeenth century Grassington Old Hall off Wood Lane, with its chapel and former fish ponds, is thought to be built on the site of a Norman house. In the thirteenth century, the Hall was owned by the Plumptons, and in 1378, John de Scardeburgh (Scarborough) was living there. In the sixteenth century it became part of the Clifford family estates.

Grass Wood, the ancient Silva Gars is recorded in 1603 as 'one in which the grass was reserved for deer', according to Dr. Whitaker (1878). Access to Grass Wood, (particularly for 'estovers', this being the rightful collection of windfall wood for fuel and of herbs for cooking), and to all the local footpaths used for centuries, has been a keenly defended issue for Grassington people. John Crowther (born in 1858), Grassington apothecary, cow doctor, antiquary and 'rights of way' defender had the interest and foresight to investigate and log the footpaths in the dale, and organised parties to walk every path in Grass Wood, after it was declared private. It is thanks largely to his devotion to this task that we are able to enjoy the freedom to wander the footpaths of this delightful green space.

The gentle walk to Grass Wood.

6 TRACKS AND TRAILS ACROSS THE MOORS

'Forget the spreading of the hideous town,
Think rather of the pack-horse on the down...'
(William Morris, The Earthly Paradise)

Tracks over the high land around Settle, Malham and Grassington are as ancient as the history of the people who once made their living there. Routes with streep gradients over the moors join the three townships and link with other roads to east and west. The course of a Roman road is thought to pass down Wharfedale to the east of the river, part of the road from Bainbridge to Ilkley, and the valley road was much later part of a coach road from London to Richmond.

Some of the green roads and tracks pass close to Iron Age hut settlements, and these tracks may be built over the earliest routes, while others visit outlying farms or lead up onto the moor tops, to sheep fells, mines or turf allotments.

Pack-horses and Drovers

The oldest through roads are often over the tops, and seem to us an arduous way of reaching the next village; however, these ways are much more direct, avoiding valleys which would be rough wooded ground, liable to flood. Sure-footed pack ponies, laden with full panniers or carrying sacks balanced on wooden frames, were able to climb and descend the steep and stony trails without too much difficulty. Drovers' flocks and herds were more easily managed on the moor routes, where there were grazing and overnight stopping places, like Dale Head farm below Penyghent.

The Monks of Fountains Abbey and Bolton Priory

The Cistercian monks of Fountains Abbey accumulated a million acres of

Over Silverdale and Fountains Fell from the top of Pen-y-ghent. Route taken by the Scottish drovers.

land around Malham Moor and Fountains Fell between the eleventh century and the sixteenth, and took over properties which it is thought were originally named by Norse farmers. Fountains' estates also included land and properties as far afield as the Lake District and Teesside.

Local tenants of the monks of Fountains and Bolton Priory mainly farmed sheep, which would be driven to granges like Kilnsey and Malham for shearing and lambing. Malham Tarn was owned by Fountains and was prized for its fish. Other Abbey 'businesses' carried on in the area were horse breeding (near Bordley) and lead mining.

The importance of monastic ownership can be seen in 'religious' names around Malham, taken from a current Ordnance Survey map:

Chapel Cave	Chapel Fell	Freer Hood
Monk's Road	Parson's Pulpit	Low Monk Leys
Monk Barn	Prior Hall	Dean Scar
Dean Moor	Dean Moor Hill	Prior Rakes
Friar Garth	Chapel Gate	Chapel House
Abbott Hills	Priest Ravine (Settle)	Priest's Tarn

In 1536, Henry VIII began to dissolve the abbeys, and the monks finally left Fountains in 1839, their lands being divided and sold.

Trails across the Moors

There are many paths, pack-horse trails and green roads in the area, and the excellent books by Arthur Raistrick and Bill Mitchell document them well. National Park Centres at Grassington and Malham and the Tourist Information Centre at Settle have useful descriptive leaflets about walks in the area. Tourist information and National Park advice about walking these routes should be followed rigorously, particularly with regard to preparation, which should be as for rough mountain walking.

Four favourite tracks with variations are now described, where travellers may care to remember the Iron Age tribes, Norse and Anglian farmers, Romans, traders, pack-drivers, monks and miners, treading before them over the moors.

Bilberry

Settle to Malham via Stockdale *(approx seven miles one way)*

This ancient pack-horse way was part of an important network of east-west trading routes,

connecting market towns and villages, and trodden by
bell-harnessed pony trains loaded with salt, wool,
hides and every commodity. Other footsteps on
this stony pass would be those of drivers of
sheep and cattle, travellers connected with the
great religious houses (the base of a monastic
cross is said to be part of the wall by Stockdale
Farm) and possibly Roman soldiers on the
march.

Further afield, east from Malham, one route
continued past Gordale over Boss Moor via
Lainger House to Threshfield and Grassington,
thence to Pateley Bridge and Ripon (along the
course of the present B6265). Other through routes
east from Malham climbed to Mastiles Lane, and on
the moor, tracks which can still be seen on the ground
connected monastic houses such as Bordley. In the other direction,
from Settle there are clear routes west towards Kirkby Lonsdale and
Lancaster.

Around one mile after leaving Settle on the steep Malham road, a
lane (not for vehicles) to the left is signposted 'Stockdale', by the
supposed site of a Roman camp. After half a mile along the lane,
spectacular limestone scenery to the left announces the proximity of
Attermire Scar and its marsh (once a lake), and Victoria Cave, an
important bone cave thought to be a pre-glacial hyena den, later used
by people of the Stone Age, Bronze Age and the Romano-British
Brigantes.

As the road rises and becomes a stony path with limestone

*Stockdale - the old road climbs to the pass. Stockdale farm and its barns can just
be seen in the far distance.*

From Stockdale Lane, wonderful limestone scenery can be seen. Altermire Scar hides its caves, and at the foot of the scar marshy ground was once Athulf's lake.

outcrops, wide views unfold west over the Ribble Valley and Forest of Bowland, and Stockdale Farm with its field barns, is passed to the right.

The farm of Stockdale is first recorded in 1160 as belonging to Sawley Abbey. The name is likely to mean 'outlying cattle farm in a valley', which perfectly describes the situation of the isolated farmstead. After the watershed is crossed, there is a choice of trails, and an energetic walker wishing to make a round trip could follow the Hoober Edge footpath route into Malham, and the Ewe Moor packhorse route out and back to the watershed.

The trail to the north east, passes the restored monastic Nappa Cross (the word 'nappa' is thought to mean a round topped hill, like an upturned bowl), which stands sentinel commanding an extensive panorama over Malham

Near the top of the pass, look back towards the forest of Bowland and Settle in the dip. Beware hungry sheep.

From Nappa Cross, the upland expanse of once monastic land includes Malham Tarn and Fountains Fell.

Tarn, Fountains Fell, Flasby Fell and Great Whernside. In the past, the cross marked the meeting point of two important tracks, a landmark seen from many miles away, as would be Weets Gate Boundary Stone near Gordale, thought to be the base and upright of a medieval cross.

The moor here is called 'Grizedales', a name associated with pigs. The old track leads to Langscar Gate and Dean Moor, (Dean being

A path descends to Malham via Hoober Edge, passing remains of mining activity and old field barns.

Arriving at Malham from Hoober Edge - follow the footpath to Beck Hall and Cove Road.

an old family name and said to be the first owner of the moor after the monks), thence to Mastiles and Kilnsey.

The forward track proceeds down Pikedaw Hill, where there are many signs of past mining activity for lead, copper and calamine, an ore of zinc, used in the making of brass, which was sold to the Cheadle Brass Company from 1795. Passing the new Calamine Shaft, sunk in 1806, the trail joins the Cove Road very close to Malham Cove, turning downhill for half a mile into Malham village.

An alternative old footpath to Malham branches off a few hundred yards after the pass, past limestone clints and grykes along Hoober Edge, and affords beautiful views of Malham village in its well-favoured sheltered spot amongst the ancient field patterns. The path descends past historic field barns into the village, emerging at Beck Hall where refreshments may be obtained by the beck.

Mastiles Lane *(Street Gate to Kilnsey, around 6 miles)*

Mastiles Lane is probably the best known and most important route over Malham Moor, the green road section being accessed by walkers at Street Gate near Malham Tarn, where there is a Bronze Age burial mound on Seaty Hill.

The name Mastells is first recorded in 1626. Some dialect meanings of the word are a bridle path, a gap in a wall and a steep path up a hill, but the most favoured is from Old English words for

A chance to do some droving.

Towards Street Gate from the Roman camp.

marsh and stile: a true description, as in wet weather the lane over Malham Moor can be virtually impassible for walkers, churned into deep water filled ruts by sport-seeking off-road vehicles whose trails stray far from the track.

This was part of a most important through route across the north of England for monastic traffic, drovers, pack-horse trains and travellers and the route can be traced from Fountains Abbey to the Lake District, where the Abbey owned land near Keswick and summered sheep there. The road ran through Pateley Bridge, Grassington and Skirethorns, and over Malham Moor, with a nearby track via Bordley (linking with Malham granges, or monastic farms and other Fountains properties). Later, its importance is shown in *Paterson's Roads* of 1812, as part of the through road from York to Lancaster.

To the east, Mastiles Lane stretches from Street Gate to Kilnsey, the most important Abbey Grange in the area. Following onward from Kilnsey, a further route ascends from Conistone via Scot Gate Lane, and Bycliffe Road to Sandy Gate and Nidderdale.

To the west, the surfaced road continues past Streets, an important ancient cross-roads for travelling between Malham and Arncliffe. Just past Capon Hall (thought to mean 'the traders' hill' in Old Norse), a branch turns off to Langcliffe and Settle, and the road continues as Henside Lane, with a branch off to Stainforth, going

Across the Wharfe at Conistone, Bycliffe Road, a continuation of Mastiles Lane, climbs over Conistone Moor. To the left is Castle Rock, and to the right the dry valley of Conistone Dib.

Monastic cross base on Mastiles Lane

forward as the rough track Moor Head Lane, to Helwith Bridge and onward through Clapham to the west. At Henside, the course of the old road from Langcliffe to Arncliffe can be followed as a footpath across Knowe Fell.

From Street Gate, east of Malham Tarn, Mastiles Lane passes over a large area of marshy ground. It is not hard to imagine the surface of this exposed moorland track churned up with the passage of pack-horse trains, travellers on foot and horse, and flocks of sheep and cattle. In the past, the track was not walled (as most of it is today) and in muddy weather the quagmire would spread out far from the route.

The windswept moor, subject to torrential storms and biting wind in the winter, hides its secrets well: who would now imagine the great summer cattle fairs of the eighteenth century, and an ale house at Great Close, a mile to the north, with another fair at Boss Moor to the south-east?

Mastiles Lane is full of interest for the walker; around Bordley

Larch

ancient paths can be followed between monastic properties, and other features are an Iron Age burial mound on Great Close Scar, a Roman camp and the nearby half-sunk base of a monastic cross, of which there is a further example by Streets.

The Monk's Road *(Street Gate to Arncliffe)*

A monastic track leads from Street Gate on Mastiles Lane in a northerly direction over the watershed into Littondale: on the Ordnance Survey map the track begins near the boathouse by Malham Tarn. This fascinating route, which was used for centuries as a pack-horse way, passes close by sixteenth century Middle House, built on the site of a Norse sheep farmstead later owned by the monks of Fountains. The isolated farmhouse, 1,500 ft above sea level, surrounded by windblown trees, almost hidden and sheltered by the hills at the head of the pass, faces away from prevailing winds and looks almost fortified, with slit windows to the path. Its small crofts, sheepfolds and dovecote are preserved, empty as if a tenant had just left. Middle House appears in earliest records (1379) as Midlow House, possibly from the Norse meaning 'meeting house', and is a further reminder of the Norse sheep farmers who settled the moor, and of the large Iron Age settlement on the nearby pasture. Lead was also mined hereabouts, on Middle House Height.

Middle House was the family home of the Knowles family, but at the census of 1841 only Jane Preston (forty-five) and George Maller (twenty) lived there. Many of the farms in the area share a similar pattern of history of Norse foundation, Abbey tenancy and sixteenth century or later rebuilding.

After passing Middle House, a branch of the path descends to Darnbrook House, another of the Abbey properties, but the main track contours the hillside, with magnificent views, past more Iron Age settlements, before descending steeply to Arncliffe.

A further green track runs north-east from Street Gate to Arncliffe Cote, more or less parallel to the Monk's Road, and may be considered for a long circular walk on a fine summer's day. The green unenclosed way winds over the huge walled field called Great Close,

and this is where the famous annual cattle fairs were held, at their height in the mid-eighteenth century, with kilted Scottish drovers bringing herds of black cattle from as far away as the Hebrides, to pasture here before being auctioned. More than 5,000 beasts could be gathered here at any one time, and their owners were able to drink at a 'house of refreshment' nearby. For food, the Scottish drovers brought their own sack of oatmeal, which would be used to make porridge in a hole in the ground - hence the name 'Porridge Stoop' in parts of the north. When they had eaten, their dogs would be allowed into the hole to finish off!

A route is clear from Malham Tarn, near the boat house.

Boss Moor to the south-east was also the site of an important fair. It was here that the wholesale traders from Great Close sold off stock in smaller lots to local farmers. The fair, with its own inn known as the Waste, saw quarrels, fights, robberies and murder, several skeletons being discovered on the moor in the nineteenth century.

Monk's Way *(Settle to Stainforth, about 7 miles return)*

An old monastic way leaves Settle by the steep and stony Banks Lane (from Castle Hill) and contours the hillside, before descending to peaceful Langcliffe, where there were once five ale houses (including the '*Naked Woman*' previously mentioned). The road continues up

Middle House stands in isolation at the head of the pass.

The green way tp Arncliffe Cote by High Mark takes in Great Close, the huge field where the grand cattle fairs were held. Up to 5,000 beasts would have grazed here at a time.

Pike Lane ('pike' being from Old English for a hill top) through to Stainforth, owned in the past by the monks of Sawley Abbey. From Stainforth Force there is a pleasant riverside walk back to Settle, for those who wish to make a round trip.

*P*OST SCRIPT

Remains of past peoples, ancient paths and ways are easily damaged. What has stood for a thousand years can be destroyed in one afternoon by churning tyres. A footpath from an ancient bridge, used by freemen for centuries can be similarly blocked and taken away from us for all time.

The north of England suited the Cistercian monks who valued solitude and peace. The quiet cattle and sheep, the moorland sweeping to the sky and lark rising, the wind bending the marsh grass, all these were known to those walking the moors before us.

Let us remember them and keep the ancient ways, and keep them quiet, so that we who also need and value peace and solitude may find refreshment for the soul.

From Winterburn reservoir, the view towards Bordley and Mastiles, with Boss Moor over to the right. This upland area was once lively with cattle fairs, horse breeding, honest dealers and rogues - now the wind whispers in the reeds.

$\mathscr{B}$IBLIOGRAPHY

Brayshaw, Thomas. *The "Borough" Guide to Settle and Giggleswick, with historical notes.* Settle, T. Tomlinson, Craven Stationery Co., 1922.

Brayshaw, Thomas and Robinson, Ralph M. *A History of the Ancient Parish of Giggleswick: Which included the Townships of Giggleswick, Settle, Rathmell, Langcliffe and Stainforth.* Halton & Company Ltd., 1932.

Brooks, Susan D. *A History of Grassington.* Dalesman Publishing Company Ltd., 1979.

Brown, George H. *On Foot Round Settle.* Settle, J.W. Lambert, 1896.

Field Studies Council. *Malham Tarn Field Centre.*

Forshaw, Chas F. ed. *Yorkshire Notes and Queries, Volumes 1 and 2.* Bradford, Henry Casaubon Derwent, 1906.

General Register Office Census 1851.

Goldthorpe, Ian. *Grassington and the Surrounding Villages Towards the Millennium.* The Dales Book Centre Grassington, 1999.

Goldthorpe, Ian. *One Hundred Things to see on a Walk through Grassington.* Seventh edition.

Grassington One Hundred, 1998.

Hargrove E. *The Yorkshire Gazetteer.* Knaresborough, Hargrove and Sons, 1812.

Harker, Rev. Bailey J. *The Buxton of Yorkshire.* Manchester, John Heywood, 1890.

Johnson, David. *Discovery Walks in the Yorkshire Dales.* Sigma, 1996.

Lofthouse, Jessica. *Countrygoer in the Dales.* Hale, 1964.

Malham: A Practical Guide for Visitors. Dalesman, 1978.

Metcalfe, Peter. *The Place-Names of North Craven.* 1985.

Mitchell, W.R. *Ghost-hunting in the Yorkshire Dales.* Castleberg, 1996.

Mitchell, W.R. *How They Lived in Old Settle.* Castleberg, 1989.

Morris, R.W. *Yorkshire through Place-Names.* David and Charles, 1982.

Muir, Richard. *Old Yorkshire: the Story of the Yorkshire Landscape and People.* Michael Joseph, 1987.

North Yorkshire County Record Office Publications. *No. 14. Sept. 1977: Tithe Apportionment, 1844. Census Returns, 1851.*

Raistrick, Arthur. *Green Roads in the Mid-Pennines.* Moorland Publishing Company, 1978.

Raistrick, Arthur. *Old Yorkshire Dales.* David and Charles, 1967.

Raistrick, Arthur. *Malham and Malham Moor.* Dalesman Publishing Company, 1971.

Riley, Frederic. *The Settle District and North West Yorkshire Dales.*

Settle: an Appreciation of Settle. Settle and District Civic Society, 1973.

Settle and North Craven. Dalesman Books, 1975.

Settle Town Trail. North Craven Building Preservation Trust.

Smith, A.E. *The Place Names of the West Riding of Yorkshire (8 vols.).* Cambridge University Press, 1970.

Speight, H. *Upper Wharfedale.* London, Elliot Stock, 1900.

Whitaker, Thomas Dunham LLD, FSA, Vicar of Whalley in Lancashire. *The History and Antiquities of the Deanery of Craven, in the County of York.* 3rd edition. Leeds, Joseph Dodgson, 1878.

Whynne-Hammond, Charles. *Tracing the History of Place-Names.* Countryside Books, 1992.

ACKNOWLEDGEMENTS

With grateful thanks to the following for their kind permission to reproduce artwork, photographs, maps, postcards and prints:

Christine Gibson, artist, for her original drawings of Craven

Hilary Maudsley of The Green, Upper Settle for permission to include illustrations from her private collection of antique postcards.

North Yorkshire County Library for photographs of Settle Market Place, Settle Cheapside & Castleberg and Grassington Square, all from Skipton Library Collection.

K. and J. Jelley, Langcliffe, Settle, Photograph of Girl on Well Hill Steps, from 'The Horner Collection' (all negatives copyright, all enquiries, telephone: 01729 822963).

Phil Hudson of Hudson History, Procter House, Kirkgate, Settle (Map of Settle 1848).

Len Atkinson of Cottingley for his photograph of The Green, Settle.

Ordnance Survey for permission to reproduce maps.

All other photographs and artwork are the author's.

I would like to thank the following people for their help and encouragement:

Ted and Philippa Holmes of Malham for much hospitality and kindness, and for access to their home library; Bill Graham for sharing his research about Giggleswick and Margaret Graham for her support and hospitality; Mrs G.M. Lawson of Giggleswick for information about the village; Phil Hudson of Hudson History (Settle), Joe and Emma Ellis, for reading and commenting on the manuscript, Liz Kidman, for information about Malham Moor, Hazel Eddon, Information Librarian, Skipton Library, for her professional advice and assistance with resources and Chris Graham for proofreading and commenting on the text. A special thank you to Mike Parsons of Wharncliffe Books for unwavering support.

Finally much thanks to my dear husband Roger for his patience, especially for waiting in teeth-chattering gales while I took photos on the tops, and to Prince, reliable trailfinder and fireguard.

INDEX